THE MYTH
OF HORIZON

THE MYTH
OF HORIZON

fractile.

Constance Hunting

ASPHODEL   PRESS
MOYER BELL LIMITED
Mount Kisco, New York & London

ACKNOWLEDGMENTS

After the Stravinsky Concert (Scribners, 1969)
Cimmerian (Puckerbrush Press, 1972)
Beyond the Summerhouse (Puckerbrush Press, 1976)
Nightwalk (University of Maine Press, 1980)
Dream Cities (ECW Press/Puckerbrush Press, 1982)
Between the Worlds, limited edition (Theodore Press, 1988)

Published by Asphodel Press

Copyright © 1991 by Constance Hunting

Frontispiece drawing by Miriam Jerison
Jacket painting by Vanessa Bell

First Edition

LIBRARY OF CONGRESS
CATALOGING-IN-PUBLICATION DATA

Hunting, Constance.
     The myth of horizon / Constance Hunting.
     — 1st edition
          p.   cm.

     I. Title.

     PS3558.U5M9   1991
     811′ .54—dc20   90-20455
                                               CIP
     ISBN 1-55921-044-3 (Pb)

Printed in the United States of America
Distributed by Rizzoli International Publications, Inc.

CONTENTS

Part One

Part Two

Part Three

I

PART ONE

THE RIDE

The white hair of the old
lady in the closed
window of the black
automobile. She sits
very straight, looking from right
to left as the car
turns the corner.
She is being taken for a ride, is it
by her son or perhaps a dutiful
middle-aged nephew.
The trees drop a few leaves in token.

Ach, the white
cotton wool
and the two grasshopper eyes
peering on stalks this way
and that.
She is helpless, she is old.
I do not want to be like that
taken for a ride by Mr. I-Don't-Know.
Keep your leaves, trees, don't write to me.

sea meadows

COMING HOME

I leave my armor by the umbrella stand and enter.
   At the first word I think of stone
      walls, sea meadows, and the sweet
         fearful smiles of old ladies in streetcars.

Blood of my blood and bone of my bone
they sit and stare me down.
His hands with tender spots of age
spread like soft meat on either knee.
"The hollyhocks this year—the salt air
brightens them, y' know. (Had you forgotten?)
What d' you have out there—
linden, is it? Immigrant shrub."
Her fingers clasp each other in the lap
where once, unborn, I must have leapt
half symbol, half embarrassment.
"We were a little disappointed—" she begins
with terrible timidity.
Love trembles in the proffered cup.
Then seedling, shifting, swelling,
sprouting, flourishing, brandishing, shaking-
shouting tree of pride, fruits pumice-
textured, clustered, shrunken,
color of never and despair—
                  but after all,
what have they done to me, what crime
committed time on time in this small room?
And my own children, yet to be?
Splay-fingered, milky-mouthed, they will of course
love me, love me, love me.

ON THE POSSIBLE KILLING OF
A THREE-MONTHS CHILD BY A RABBIT

Was it raining, did the street lights bleed
rosy haloes through the city mist?
The weather might be important.
Was it a beautiful night?
Oh, the red eyes, oh, the vibrissa
hanging over the raddled couch.
And the fur, like cotton candy, like the ghost of the
                    biggest
snowman.
Where did it grow, how did it get itself
out of the cage, out of the newspapers?
It was someone's pet, for God's sake?
WHO WAS THE FRIEND?
The father snores.
I knew a lady once pulled out
her eyelashes by the roots.
She was tall as a poplar,
pale as an ash.
Did the flesh
taste sweet, like new lettuce leaves,
wild onions, milky as white rose petals?
From the little stump a rubbery string
drools like the shred
of a red balloon. Sleep, baby.

TRANSFERENCES

This is my year for looking
ironically beautiful.
People respond to me.
What big eyes I have!

They are glass.
Such glossy hair,
it is made of damp chestnut leaves.

My skin has the fashionable
pallor of arsenic.
And that fine-boned nose!
Precisely.

Ego is a malodorous weed.
Such long nails!

AFTER THE STRAVINSKY CONCERT

i

Introduzione:

*voce
principale*

One day the pier glass in the entrance hall
swayed slightly, shuddered, and slid down the
    wall.
Just so an aunt of mine
was found once, sitting on the parquetry
in the same place near dawn, her wreath awry
and roses on her breath; but that perhaps
is neither here nor there, the glass uniting both
having long since been carried to the lumber-
    room,
leaving us nothing to reflect upon.
The gilded frame
was loosened and the mirror cracked. A cherub
    lost
a flying ribbon and whatever
had been underneath was only plaster.

ii

*Larghetto
indeciso:*

vocina

Fell of its own weight was the verdict I knew
    better
girl though I was then, not yet risen
from the kitchen where that afternoon
the dishes rattled like the bowels
of a starving man they said along the gallery
the pictures swung as if freshly hanged
and in the drawing-room the vases chattered
like nervous women in a thunderstorm—
it was the boys
old men now stuffed with honors till their eyes

bulge out as if already marble
noble this and noble that on Sundays
glossy in the sups you might have seen
my photo too last birthday toothless I looked
but at least alive—I was saying
the nephews jumping on the beds upstairs
that was the cause. Your grandmother
was fond of them Lord alone knows why fond-
foolish if you ask me or else proud
to be bewildered so.
They should never have been invited at all.

iii

*Andante
sostenuto:*

voce
principale

Not half an hour before the fall, my grand-
        mother
had stood impaling with the perfect calm
of confidence in time and place her floating hat
upon a pin; perfectly gentle, perfectly good,
pierced thus the instant, crowned herself
innocent patroness of place and time.
This was her afternoon to call.
The mirror gave her back her face
wondrously like: she knew
exactly where she was within the frame,
could lift a gloved finger if she wished
to touch the earlobe where the pearldrop
        sprung
chaste fruit of gold, and what she saw
she touched could feel, by sense and reason
mirror-assured that touch and sight were one,
aspects of distance and the moment joined
in a grave image of reality, as if she had been
        swan
and glass the stilled
water she moved on, making a single silvered
        self
(liable, however, to current and the wind

shaking the silvered surface of the dream).
When she came home, here the great boys had
        been
and had their game. She did not scold; said
        merely
she had been fond of it; had it put away.
The frame, she said, might someday be of use.

iv

Scherzo,
mancando
poco a poco:

voce
principale

The house stayed wide, the gardens blowing
garlands of light and roses through the open
        doors,
the lawns with blandly insolent grace unrolled
in green chiaroscuro to the little lake
below the pavilion where the spoilt peacocks
        screamed
for tidbits from the luncheon guests who
        strolled
in clothes appropriate to the view.
Beyond, the ground-flowers in the meadows
        fairly
hiccupped out of the grass, and the gilt-edged
        sun
beat like a gong about the rooks all summer
        long
wheeling and wheeling in the burnished sky.
We never saw it that way.
Something had altered by the time we came,
something we could not put a finger on
but felt insensibly the absence of
had been withdrawn; some force which would
        surround,
protect, make fast a floating present; stay
the nettle and keep out the rot.
The place seemed at loose ends.
When we first found the pier-glass in the
        lumber-room

we were amused a while to see how true
had cracked so easily to false, or, it might be,
from false to true; and minced and mimed,
though Reba, the youngest, held up, cried:
her nose was flawed like her old doll's.
The game queered, we slammed outside.
The sky was threatening somehow; had
      crazed,
turned tarnished, and at the last
let down its brittle rain.
We sat against the wall and watched
the season going under in the fall.

v

Finale:
grave assai:

coro

This is November of no beggars riding,
no more strawberries and cream, when Babylon
is gone out with the candle and the seam
is none too fine. Night descends early now,
it's hard to tell the substance by these shadows.
The thin wind blows hey moaney o,
fragments and shards! fragments and shards!
No nonnies, no nannies, no go, lovely rose.
We sit against the wall and stare
into the splintering of air.

REVENANT

i

The day my father died in burning fall,
pyres were lit all up and down the streets;
and on the afternoon I saw his recent ghost
it came—no more a Lucifer
than any other man's or Faustus either—
it came, again I say, upon the haze
hung like a summer's cerements
thick and sententious in the anxious air.
But he came quick, familiar glint
of calmly humorous inquiry
a nick in the corner of his eye.
Windows were open, I was playing
unaccustomed Chopin in the mist
that smoked the mirror, made the cat cough
and curled the fern's fingers back towards dust.
Had I been playing Bach
I doubt my father would have come,
for, as it happened, he had only one
piece to his name,
almost the slowest Prélude in the book,
single survivor of surly Saturday mornings
chopped into little pieces by the clock
while in his brain the spit-lovely, curving ball
arced purely, maddeningly, through seraphic blue.

ii

Surely the teacher stayed, let alone returned,
solely because of my grandmother's coffee,
deep, strong, and bitterly bracing,

support, so she claimed, for the silver spoon
dipped by the innocent into the red-gold brew
this clattering tall witch brought with the steam
still on it, fresh from her chivvying.
The boy slipped out and ran towards his own way.
I knew the parlor well, from childhood summers on.
Cool, high-ceilinged, rosewood, mahogany,
words over memory like a chime: here shall they sit,
be summoned up and wound, submit once more,
the foreign, patient master with his awkward shoes
primly together under the dark plush pall,
the talking woman with her full blue eyes
flashing out kindness as it were argument.
The table between them's firm as the equator.
Beside these curios, those in the what-not dim
(even the giant conch, borne back a trophy,
pink as a god's other ear, from Atlantic City
and my grandparents' wedding trip).
                                        She lets him off
before he grows too weary, but she does not fail
to note the exhaustion of his drooping cuffs.
It does not matter that I never saw him.
He wore a pince-nez, parted his thin gray hair
in the center, had a trick
of pressing his finger-ends as though in prayer;
lived in one room above the post office,
had no piano, practised at the church;
cared overmuch for beauty considering
his means and his existence; died
weightless, smiling ambiguously, and left no will.
And yet my father learned his piece.

iii

Ontario springs are rain-flogged out of winter's
chilblained grip. Ice boomed
and buckled on the Chippewa, the puck
skidded, striking rime in sprays; girls screamed,

scarves streaming red like February dawns,
as the whip snapped and skirts went flying
showing a tingling glimpse of wrinkled cotton shins.
By late March the ice was used up, yellow,
and willows took the yellow towards their green.
You had to watch the rotted wooden sidewalks
as, burbling with tonic, challenging the cracks,
you swaggered out adolescent as the season.
From the veranda, Emma and Maud waved Saturday
dustcloths and shouted something rude.

They were the older sisters, Allegra next,
Bertha the baby. My father was nearly christened Paul,
indeed was called so for his first few months,
but my grandmother changed her mind the week before
the ceremony; she had no time to read
except while nursing, and that year
it was Goethe (in translation), so it was John
anglicized and wailing in his lace-trimmed robe
who was sprinkled the only son instead.

My grandfather was in groceries,
natural gas, washing machines, lord knows,—
a Personage with a capital,
the cock of his hat, the lilt of his moustache,
the heft of chain across his vest told that.
Raised in the midst of presbyters,
he backslid gradually from divvying
the children with his Anglican
on alternate Sundays to the porch
hammock and counting ruby-throated
hummingbirds while, very black-and-white,
very erect, she set out trailing charges
like a swift silken kite. "Fifty-six
at service," she would report, and he
respond, "Eleven at the trumpet vine."

One day they take the boat to Buffalo,
he has a man to see; she has the stores,

of course, and asks no questions, being here,
and only here, diffident. They arrange to meet
at 2 p.m. at a monument they both like.
She is there. She is there a good hour,
grown very tall, moreover, and beset
by pigeons. "Tommy," she says in a voice
of thinnest glass, "where have you been?"
"I've been flying," says Grandfather, "all over Buffalo
with Sir Harry Oakes in his private plane.
He found it was my birthday." And settles his chin
onto his collar with absolute éclat.
He took five teaspoonsful of sugar in his milk,
but it was Russian rubles did him in at last.

His mother lived along another street.
John was her favorite. A little boy
in knickers with a devilish bright eye
he stood behind her chair in hottest June
and fanned her heaving, purple chest.
Immensely old, immensely fat, she fought
the ostrich feathers with her jagged breath
and wheezed against her fancied ills,
slightings by relatives, stealing by kitchen girls,
asthmatic whispers coiling in his ear
like the fierce distant thunder in a shell.
Still he was fascinated, even when
as it were between complaints she gave a sudden gasp,
clutched at eluding air, and went right under.
It was the silence, not her final glare,
fixed and affronted, freed his howl
and flung the fan down at her slippered feet
and sent him thudding home to beggar noise.
The following week he drowned
Allegra's coral brooch in the sulphur well
and was soundly strapped. His sobs
were loud with gratitude.
Was taught to swim by being rowed
to the river's middle, harnessed to a rope

and tossed in; down he sank
thrashing like any sunny into the rank
muddy whorls, and rose up gagging
for his pa's laughing under his panama;
his father hauled him in hand over hand,
tossed him again, again; until
the boy glistened and panted like a tadpole
and took the other element for pleasure granted.
The sun was staggering on the western slope
when the pronouncement came: "Now you can swim,"
the tamer said, and lit a fresh cigar.
The boy never doubted it was true.
One wet, one dry, they headed for the shore
where Emma flapped the supper semaphore.

iv

A gloss of days: one guesses, one must guess.
In the upstairs hall there hung a length of frame
entitled *Life's High Moments*. After the bassinet,
hooded like a snuffer, and the child
velvet-suited, banged, and guarded by
the Saint Bernard whose tongue lolled sweetly out,
a young gentleman in faultless evening clothes
correctly bowed before a maiden piled with hair.
The next panel showed the wedding, she
impenetrably veiled, and after that
they got into the carriage and were driven off.
And then? And then? We do not know.
We are not apprised. We imagine gone
what we are not sure existed even once—
school fights, bad dreams, the poster pointing
you to fight the Huns: the night the horse was tied
to the banister on the second floor
of Croyden House; free-lance experiments
in foggy fields, knowledge the premised province—
it receded, rather. . . . And all this, all these
gone by and hardly reconciled

with what has come, and been, and gone again.
I enter late,
with other burdens, into smaller rooms.
The dimpled moon that drew you by her smile
into her sphere outlasted you
and now sinks sidewise with her numbing grin
hugely enspreading whatever face you loved.
Can I restore you to a simpler tune
than that which wrangled out our times that mingled
making the players fret and mumble too?
It is dusk now. Do not light the lamp.
Let the place be neutral, somewhere between
my haunted present and your haunting pale.
Peace to the footfall, rapid and sentient;
let be resolved and recognized lost seasons; wait
for the steady, lifeless breathing of the snow.

THE GATHERING

Evening: At Table

I have remembered sense of generations
packing in close about a feast of time
as though existence were a dining table,
we the invited guests, and I a child again
and pressed between the two tall bony aunts
whose silk skirts spill along my skinny shanks,
whose heads like weedy flowers nod
emphatically across me on their stems
showing the stringy tautened cords
attaching them to Sundays such as these.

Summer. Evening. The dark-veined honeycomb
of glass, the colored dome to childish eyes
a marvel is slid downward on its chain
and sheds its colors as it comes
to harlequin us all. Features stand out
suddenly: an older uncle will begin to look
like his own mother as she looked in age;
his wife will give her maiden name away
in her hand's shape, as if a common line
were written in her palm,—
a dozen like it gesture down the row.
Light falls upon a cheek as it did years
ago for someone else,
and little Shelagh's got the double crown.
We pass our plates up for the victuals,
talking the whole time, or the grown people do,—
interspersed others clutch soft silver spoons

teethed over long since by their elders;
eager in bibs, and propped, they lean
forward and breathe, and slobber slightly,
dazed by the noise, the smells, the light.
(A missing few went earlier to bed,
netted about in hasty cots to listen to
the last birds meting out a day
so brief it must have seemed the sun
opened its eye once fully, gazed gold, then
drowsed it closed again with theirs
and let the mottoes fade upon the wall
and vines and roses over them grow fast
in flowing dark, and cover up
their names.)
Outside, the moths beat furious at the window screen.
The lamp above us glows its blood-
red, blue, its brooding green;
but while the voices rise,
I see my mother sitting silent, pale,
skewered to pride and shyness by her cameo.

ii

Evening: The Mother

She sits stiff, crumbling bread, the smile
stretched tight upon her linen face.
Talk tires her, she often says.
Her rages are so private that they've bleached her gaze,
held lowered now lest it should show
dread or revulsion of the human tribe
she's been betrayed to. Oh, she is cold,
she cannot stand the draught
coiling round her shoulder. She is dry,
as though some spring were sealed from birth,
yet she can weep. She can weep.
Children she loves most when they sleep

or are ill; no one is then kinder,
gentler, more solicitous. Children when they sleep
must be covered; must not thrash; when ill
may be cared for tenderly; otherwise
must be punished gravely, else discover sin,
which will result in telling lies.
Stay still, she murmurs in her whitened tone,
lie down now; sleep. And goes a shade
of white out of the dusky room.
The child stares fearful into dark,
not knowing why. I will not know
till later what sleep means to her.

iii

Morning: The Grandmother

Long ago
this morning,
flattening myself
against my spine, I try
the top stair.
It makes no outcry, so I test
the next, and it receives me too.
The third step creaks
loudly; it makes a hole
in silence. I draw my foot back just in time
and wait, but the hall
above gives no sign; sleep
still holds them up there in a milky mist.
And I go on, picking my way,
my passage down
to seven o'clock of a fine
midsummer dawning past its rosy wake
and gone to flower within
the oriole window of the hall below.
I follow

clues: the cloudy cape
cowled on the newel post, daubed gloves
damp on silver tray, wet trail along parquet,
and chestnut-colored odor
curling beneath the kitchen door. Aha!
My father's mother, tall, hawk-
nosed and vigilant, has of course made the grand
first tour of the day.
Of the garden. In her man's
straw hat, and galoshes left
by some unremembered guest, and bearing
the flat wicker basket and the shears just as
sharp as mercy, she has visited
her stations; paused
to weed, to snip, to let in air about the roots;
and now, her apron on, the vases out,
poses at the counter, parrying
snapdragons!
Oh, it's you!
she says, and, Good: you can pit cherries.
But I don't know
how, I whine. She
shows me how my thumb can pop
the pit out neat as an eyeball. Charmed,
I set to work, we set to work.
"Juice makes a cherry," says the woman wisely,
sticking in stalks
pendent with bloom. "I wouldn't give a fig
for a cherry without juice."
We laugh easily together.
Shaping the day between us, our wrists run
with warmth, the quickness, the sweet light.

iv

Noon: The Grandfather

I am a lady now for solitude and green
wavering light at parlor French
long windows sunk in vines.
Armchair grandeur! Splendor of rose-
wood and mahogany, and don't forget
the faded Turkish carpet on the floor,
the mends don't show.
I pull a book whose leather flakes
like dried leaves from the shelf.
Happens it's Shakespeare, as I like it,
me, myself, some Rosalind
half-boy, all brave new world,
Miranda, root: to be wondered at, and lost
in profound reality, I reel a little, and read on.
"A dreadful light
to see by," says my prosperous
grandfather's voice from the doorway:
fingering the gold
chain across his vest, he makes his choice,
advances to the piano stool, and sits,
knee cocked jaunty over
other, Sabbath trouser leg. Oh, the swell
his prideful belly makes in person and in place.
You'd think he embodied half the globe.
I do not quarrel with that. I admire
his black magic broadcloth and his milkweed hair.
He smells of Yardley's, wears a boutonnière,
he counts
his children's children like his dividends.
He describes a half turn on his axis,
shoots his cuffs and flexes
manicured fingers over the yellowed keys,

that tumble to his touch like dominoes.
Shower of notes, pattern of ivory tune
woven into leaves that tremble each
a listening, veined, lady's lobe to tease.
"D' you know
what tune that is?" he asks, not stopping
playing, and I hazard Sunday-wise,
"A hymn?" He chuckles. "Not a bit of it.
'Old Black Joe,' with variations. . . . Ha!"
Not stopping yet, but softer, "Had a colored
handyman once, name of Teller. Simple-
minded, but a wizard with the hoe.
Teller confused me with God. Got so
your grandmother called me that to him.
'God wants the radishes thinned. God wants
the bay hitched up, He has to see a man.'
One day the tool shed caught fire. Teller yelled.
'Get God and send a bucket!' Shack gutted.
Teller only said God moved too slow."
"And did she ever call you God after that?"
Diminuendo and amused, "You know,"
he says, "she never did."
And musing, slows, bemused,
stops. "Perhaps that was just as well."
His smile is not for me. "It is the cause,
my soul. . . . What was his wife's
name? Daisy. Yes." Light and quick shadow play
across his face. The tall black clock lets fall
eleven wafers into the crack of time.

V

Noon, Afternoon: Relatives

Uncle Johnny comes just then,
dares to ask if that's too soon,
one eye blue and one eye brown,

hand out always, grin turned on,
plunks him down and starts to croon
how his wife has left again.
How I love my uncle John.

Twin
ancients, sisters in their skin
and bone
of bone, but somehow
fleshless in their scrawn,
sit side by side in lady
chairs and bleed disdain.
High thoughts have drawn their tempers thin.
Dried lips are formed to speak
a no, or yawn.
They have forgot, if ever they have known,
how seldom is a goose mistook for swan.
Is there no beauty here? Yes, in she comes,
bearing the rosy garland of her afternoon
that has not yet begun to wane:
pranced after by her two young blooms,
two variants of a single stem
so smooth, so slender as to seem
new-sprung, although the lines
like light thorn-marks have, in the light,
begun to show beneath those beaming eyes
that shed light like twin prodigals of love.
Her husband walks a pace behind.
"Father!" she says, and stoops
to conquer that old bastion with a kiss,
"Now, Eva," he says, skittish, pleased.
"I saw you only yesterday."
And pats her bottom as a fond papa will.
Her husband glares.
He cannot help it that he looks so pale,
as if he lives forever in the shade.

I look at her, and she is like a swan.

Night: At Table

I float on swirling waters, laughter, voices,
I twirl a silver spoon.
My eyes burn, my head throbs with heat and noise,
but that's all right.
But all the faces look alike,
I hear a tune that runs along my brain,
it recapitulates itself and runs a-new.
It turns me in the whirlpool of a yawn.
And, "Time to go!" My father's voice. He
gathers me, almost hauls me up and away
from light, from the light, the rainbow-shed
blossoming, the giant flower that sways
above our table and our day and days.
"Good-night! Good-night!"

Later,
awake in the electric dark,
I hear the voices underneath the stars,
departing wheels, the calls, "Good-night!"
Footsteps on stealthy stairs.
And later still the faint click of slow heels
from outside, down on the portico
where the original hosts, arm in familiar arm,
pace like forgiving ghosts,
like the ghosts they will become.
Their guests have all gone home.
He throws away the end of his cigar,
and they go in. Gone home.
The house sighs once, and settles.
Out there, trees stir.
Sap rises in me, and I dream.

AFTERNOON OF A CONTEMPORARY POET

The friend who has a gall bladder
phones: the operation to be done
on Saturday. But only look—
the grand piano, suffering what indignities,
is rolling up the walk,
supported by three men. Crack crack
and crack the floor says, terrified.
"Do all floors do this in all houses
where you deliver pianos?"
"No, lady."
My son arrives from school, bearing a few
sad fallen leaves (it has rained since)
which we must enter immediately in
the dictionary. It is quite full already,
but he does not mind that. And out of these
will spin the tenuous free-wheeling web
of image, while from the top
of the refrigerator the Siamese,
vulture-like, brooding on fancied wrongs,
stares like the ultimate metaphor at five o'clock.

MUSING IN NEW ENGLAND:
THE LONG LAST DAY OF MRS. EDDICOMBE

". . . and stepping from thy Father's house har-
nessed a golden chariot, and the strong pinions of
thy two swans fair and swift, whirring from heaven
through mid-sky, have drawn thee towards the
dark earth. . . ."

> Sappho: "To Aphrodite"
> translated by J. M. Edmonds

". . . Ah! when the ghost begins to quick-
en. . . ."

> W. B. Yeats: "The Cold Heaven"

i

That morning opening
her eyes, cold from the sea-
damp night and seeing Day
again so clearly writ across the
curtains, Mrs. Eddicombe,
a lady of these parts, no longer young
(pluckings of dead
gray hair by dawn on the anxious pillow)
and never beautiful, however vain
(an arch of foot, a turn of wrist
were once admired; she married him
but kept the money in her name
had her two sons, and buried him,—
his actual services
were private, causing talk,
benched wit branched village-green
between hawk and spit
having it that he simply disappeared,
blew away, gone to seed at last

in that cliff-hanging garden up there, or,
wraith of a blithe
adventurer, lit out, West maybe,
past Albany: his stone,
stricken with gull-droppings, leans
anyhow in the churchyard, CAPTAIN
the granite legend reads, ay-uh)
speaks on a sudden out of dream-disordered sleep: *"Is it time?"*
Receives no answer, has expected none,
not knowing what it is she's asked,
and turns her face away from light.
Something she has been doing now for years.
Must struggle up, to stand upon the mat
and get her bearings. For the floor tilts.
And what old man
stares back at her from silt-encrusted glass?

ii

The slow stair rail unwinds
beneath her sliding palm. The landing window
gives upon the sea. If it is fine
weather, the sea is blue,
if not, the sea is gray.
The weather is fine today.
Mrs. Eddicombe is going down.
As she descends,
the sun through native bull's-eye
shoots such an arrow into her back!

That other witch has come.
She always comes
thank-God early, hobbling on her knobs,
bringing up with her village mist,
heaving the gate,
crushing the oyster shells to grit
(her husband beats her when he drinks,
red as a lobster claw). As to pearls,

pshaw! The rusted key
scrapes seven in the lock.
                              In her cave
she slams pots, chips
blue enamel, works in steam,
issues to empty slops
over the cliff, or hang
the dishrag on the lilac bush.

While in the passage, needle's eye,
the mistress, having lost the thread,
searches along the verdigris-
stained wall for traces of a name.
She hooks her father's cloak
down from its peg that sticks
an admonitory finger out
through moss or mold,
and drapes its holey folds
about her bones. Endure,
endure! She has,
she will. Only, she feels the cold
more than she used to do, and the new
throbbing of a wound she thinks is old.

                         iii

The formality of walking down the path!
Toad under dock
leaf does not stir.
Why should he budge for this tall shade
that scarcely casts a breath?
Her spells have all run out.
He stays securely under warts
and hides his jewel. A critic's stratagem.
The garden seeds itself, and has this time.
A monstrous cabbage like a coarsened rose
blooms in the lily bed, defiant dreams
a king. Salt dreams. She makes her way

among the golden droppings of the sun,
the silver spittle of the snail.
To come to stone
set like a ruined throne at cliff's edge.
Here she sinks
down, fiddles with her fancy's mourning
thoughts, cedars grow close, and wild
birds coolly cry.

iv

Limpet-born to rock
of woman gone like foam
so soon she never was
remembered, that long time ago
a creature opened,
ignorant of whether eye
or mouth or genital,
but heard the ocean in her father's voice.
Ran free in meadows,
built on sand, went with the wind,
came in to cold, and winter's rheum.
Drank smoke from the chimney.
Somewhere in her father's cups
was introduced to rhyme.
Ah! Scribblings in the eaves,
her breath a freezing cloud
(like water struck from stone),
shadows of metaphors
hung soft as bats among the rafters.
Force brought her out with her
tell-tale finger.
Malevolence
sprung from a black umbrella
shook drops of warning in her father's face
and she found the burrs dragged from her hair
and herself in a tumbril
traveling at terrible speed

into exile, pelted
by mildewed gloves and the smell of pomade
and made to learn her catechism: female.
She never got used to that country.
She got out of it as quick as she could.
But some weakness clung,
and on top of that the old man died
of a brain swelling or a cracked heart
she imagined, and saw him unforgiven
sheeted on the tide.
High and dry
in the pale dune grass she spies upon
the young men
alien as earthly
gods with water-dropleted hair
and their girls in beach-head positions
drilling in the sandy hills.
Her body like a hollow shell. Will no-one come?
She swears she will make flutes
of all the blades within her bone-dry reach.
Will no-one come?
Foam sits the ocean like the ghosts of ghosts.

v

Her hand beats pitted stone.
She lifts her hand against the light
and gazes at it, wondering what leaf
it reminds her of, altered by air
to wafer flesh. It may fall, it may fall.
Her eyes fill, not with tears
but with ice. So many seasons
in one body! That has borne
the weight of bodies, nomad tenants,
hardly received, hardly nourished,
her fault, her flaw, her unnaturals.
Even her heat then was cold.
When her first was born

she moaned for a pencil.
The second was her favorite.
Till two he spoke no word, and then said,
                    "Light!"
At three he looked into her eyes
and said, "Black suns!"
She thinks now he was right,
and smiles a smile she does not know.
At five he gave up metaphor
and joined the other at his grub-dirt games.
She gave them up, and left off feeling warm.
Soon they all treated her like glass,
talking round her, through her, breathing rough
when she froze, but never splintered her,
just vanishing like early frost from pane.
The first bred earthworms in another part
of the country, but the second stayed
to invent a telescope that counted dust.
He had the attic room
till he was committed to a lower roost.
She cleared
his room out, sat her down
and wrote his death to life.
                    So it began,
or ended, the long
betrayal, the long withdrawal—she fell
onto words like spears,
pricked herself time on time like spindles.
She bled rose-red ice.
She in her tower,
and that other
in her cave. Their spells did not collide
but they were in cahoots all the same.
Collusion wound like spider's hair
around the moldings, up the stair.
It came and went like the sea-air
under doors. *Women, we are women here,*
it whispered. *We make monsters in dry wombs,*

out of the lime we blow from men's dead bones.
Outside, the ocean laughed and muttered in his beard.

vi

Did she sleep? Nod off
in the manner of the old?
It is already quite late.
Some wind forked like a snake's
cool tongue out of the pines
touches her through her shawl.
The sea below is purpling now,
shaking itself like the hem
of the dusk's garment. That is beautiful.
This stone is very hard.
She feels as if it holds her down,
as if she has been buried sitting up
and the earth turned inside out.
She has eaten nothing the whole day,
she could die here
for anyone's care! That is the way,
that is the way of the world.
The saddest phrase. She whimpers.
She must go in. Which way is home?
By the owl's cry, she cannot tell.
She stands. Lost, lost! The sun has gone,
the moon is brewing silver from the sea,
and who, and who will have the last word?
Under his leaf, the toad chuckles in his sleep.

vii

That night, she dreams.
She has been fetched out of dark,
brought back, fed like a child
at the kitchen table. Or was that
dreaming, too? She is sure
she cried and bit the spoon.
She is sure she is lying

in her bed, has long since
heard the shell's farewell,
the white wind
die. The sea asserts its hush,
hush. Curtains
bow once and retire. The night stands wide.
Is it mice gnawing she hears,
moss growing phosphorescent on the walls?
Old houses creak and sigh.
She cannot
uncross her hands from her withered breast.
A board, a bone snaps in the hall.
Light grows in dark if it is rotten.
This rot is dry, and light.
She feels her nails lengthen.
Her tongue stretches, labors: bursts.
A stroke of time, all arching anguish,
thrashing, come, she comes,
the most exquisite. . . .

viii

And love, words, love, her eyes
have startled into stone.
Father, forgive.

ix

Incantatory

Come again come
come all forbidden words
stars beauty flowers even love
put off disguises rise to me
press shells upon my eyes
that I may wake to night or dawn
but not this everlasting lidless nooning
breathe breathe rosy breathing lightly roar
against my parched ear that I may

not die as I have been here on my rock
exposed my tongue turned bitter root
that used to ripple out sound delicate with rime
into the time that had always something of morning
now who will comb
such kelped hair
like dried blood so it cannot hear
and such a dead
sea there dies daily hourly direly
oh I am drying in this sun
I watch the unveiled sky for a flight of swans

REVELATION

My grandfather once saw a black-
snake in the act
of swallowing a frog.
Quick as lightning Grandfather
fetched the axe,
smote that snake like thunder.
The frog sprang out and sprang away
across the meadow—likely to start
a new religion. Grandfather said
you never saw a frog
leap so high!

CÉZANNE

The man astonished all of Paris
with an apple
but his wife
liked only Switzerland and lemonade.

HABITANT

Some people move about the world so easily
flying from the room that is
London to the lawn
of Vermont
to sit on whose terrace
when for an evening drink and exclaim
at which sunset
whereas
if I lived
in an attic with a cot
and a table only I would rise
stumbling and bang into every
day at the same time

FOR LUCY, TO EARTH

She who was
so tuned to light
now must lie so
stilled and mute,
who sped headlong
towards the day, the child
and instrument of sun
scarce mounted on the morning
air before
cast down to early
night and silencing of song, now lies
headlong in such dark.

She will need less
space than most,
Earth, in your partitioned place.
We can almost guarantee
she will prove
a gentle guest; mannerly
she always was, though young
in human company. She will not disturb
what's here. Earth, be gentle:
she will stay
lightly in this
stranger home.

CIMMERIAN

Cimmerian: one of a mythical people described by
Homer as dwelling in a remote realm of mist and
gloom.

i

The slow disintegration of the mind
is worse than sudden madness for the seeing,
that wraps the dreamer at a single stroke
away, away! and has the drowning done
too rapidly for fullest knowing.

To watch the water
fouled of that pure intercourse
of thought with image breaking into word
that leaps with wit the colored thread
tying the curving form to being,
and the mind

pulled slowly taut, too taut, too slow
and dredging out
dripping and heavy some poor muddish thing
to flop it panting on the bank
and slyly smile it towards
the still-sought approval,—

hello
hello
hello
say the nearly dead eyes,
the dying cornucopia mouth.
I cannot answer them,
I am weaving a wreath of hooks.

Born untimely into May
this poor lady suffered cold
and she will go out, it seems,
in the same time
in the same way,
for she is dying of it slowly,
slowly,
with a pressure on her brain,
a glacier spreading over
matter of her mind. Was she then made
for snow, or rain?
                                    She wept,
I remember that
she did weep, her secret told
for those who cared to look
next morning in the heavy fold
of eyelid, swollen pulse at throat
like birdsong turned
sullen to ice. Is it of that stoppage
she is dying, also?
What did she want, beyond the lack of ill?
Need, to be brought to this
white immaculate
tight-sheeted private bed in this private room
where even the TV screen stays blank?
Maybe she's comfortable: outside translucent
veins siphon off
soiled yellow fluids from her body's vessel,
keeping her organs clear as God's eyes
washed by the death of slaughtered innocents.
She wanted sleep. Remember,
I remember that. She longed for sleep
like love.
                    That first day
I returned, she rose up

at my entrance
quite off her bed
and gave tongue to terror
Aagh aagh aagh
That was genuine If you want to see
your mother alive the other said
over the wire you had better come
at once I saw
what was meant She fell back, and my self
went round some corner.

                        I sit beside the bed,
child to the mother, older child,
and watch her sleep
that is like sleep and yet not sleep,
deeper than sleep yet not
yet deepest sleep while breath
snores along plastic pipes
with a yellow rattle, and the shutter of skin
flickers over the eye-
ball empty of dream and of reflection
dull, a mirror badly silvered
A sleeping beauty, lying, lines I knew
on brow, at lips, gone,
cheeks plumped with false
health, rosy even, prompting
numb wonder, simplest regret.
He, at the other side,
stretches out thumb like thorn to touch (horror) her nose!
"Get out of here," he growls,
and shakes his lion's mock mane,
"and I'll buy you a new hat,"
he murmurs. Booby! Tenderness
almost breaks him down.
He turns towards me. He begs,
"Take her hand. She likes
it when you hold her hand."
My cold hand
creeps across the coverlet

to hers, I take
her warm lifeless blanched
hand, wrinkled and soft as though by soap
and long water immersion, in my own.
Such courage! I'd soonest
stroke a live
leaf that a snake kisses in passing.
I hold on.
"You think she knows?"
The snore. "She knows,"
he repeats, stubborn in love,
in self-reproach, in agony. In tears.
"She recognized you."
Yes. She did.
He leans to her. "Sweetheart."
A tone
of voice I never heard before but coming
from some love-letter past.
So, they were young once.
What else could be new?
They strolled beneath green showers of leaves,
he in blazer, she in white lawn, and I
cast the merest shadow in between.
Atone, atone.

iii

Whereas in fever fire
strikes me with its streams,
thought like a bright rippling
chain of snakes uncoils,
dazzles,
unbraiding hissing in my heightened
brain, blinds and cracks
over me its whips of deadly
play, ashes and metal
spitting from its tongues

so that I hoop myself
and stammer under beauty twinned
with terror in a killing rain,

now stand I fixed
by faulted love and colder
grief, helpless to charm
or tame, but drawn
under the goad of guilt that is
disordered
pride to finally fondle
grief
like asps to scape the gaze
of little lidless eyes
unblinking in the passing
shade of love: pride's darling
is brought down in fiery poisoned light.

iv

Once when I was a child in fever
near a winter sunset, she climbed the narrow stair
to gleam, quick and modest, in my room
with my supper tray, the evening
newspaper tucked beneath her arm
(the freckled arm summer and winter round
and strong of a country girl despite
her weekly marcel and her genteel air;
the arm that Monday meant to hang out clothes
beautifully pegged to stretch the city
backyard to a snapping breeze, and did,
so that on Tuesday nights fresh sheets towards sleep
smelled of the silver iron as of dreams
and the sanest, cleanest sun,—
her washes were her miracles, she felt that pull
of art, and in her extreme
illness, while she was still at home
at home, my father, returning at six

one January day (he clung
to the normal routine; God knows
what she did when he was away) found her
wrestling in freezing dark
with an icy sheet like a white Styx or angel,
she winning, wearing
her dead farmer brother's overcoat, and grinning,—
of course there was more to it than that).
She came into my room
mine was a little room
it faced the West
it was a little room
but it was the best
they told me I hated it
mine was the smallest room,
not a tower.

"See the bright sunset,"
she said, and I understood a truce,
a pause in our lives' occupations,
and I looked
out of my fever's tired heat and saw the red
flaring strands spread live across the sky
out my window like high stretched membrane.
"Yes," I said. Whose was it,
drying out there in the cold?
Less did I see it, less that it was bright
than bloody, wind-inflamed, more than bright,
and which sank, sun like Jehovah's streaming eye
or earth its daytime moon?

I said Yes
often in those days.
She moved my burnt-out books,
Three Musketeers, The Snow Queen, Nancy Drew,
settled the tray, gave me the news.
"The old King is dead."

George V that would be,
in the shade of Mary.
Her eyes even then washed pale
blue stones, she still
because I was ill
(no one kinder then I have told, more gentle)
made cheerful speech, so that I thought
it must be indeed a fine thing
to be a king, and die
in the red winter sunset. *Pax,*
she put her nerve-thinned hand
on my forehead that felt skinned
by fever, and enmity
in the hollow died, love, long live the dead
long live
love live the dead
roses are red but white
too her veins ran cold
as that king died by fire
her ice communicates
I will be fierce and she
will die true.

v

It is light late now. Doves in evening
moan in rooftrees, smoothing
the last rough edges from the day.
Housewives have gathered white lilac from hedges,
swept doorsills, wished they could sweep the grass,
set children out like plants and brought them in
again against the treacherous early chill.
We have risen above all that.
We cannot get up and go down there.
We must wait up here within walls for somebody.
The little bell tings
a stone flung into a river of stale air
brings tidings to our sheltered, sour air

of lives smartly cracked or pried tenderly
from shells of soft creatures we shall never touch.
The little bell stings with its reminders.
Somewhere in firehouses men sit suspendered,
doors open, hunched over unyielding checkerboards.
An old woman in a clean dress has watered her
                              African violet,
and a child cries out unheard from a dream of lions.
When can we descend to their level?
Pulled tight like ineffectual angels
on our plastic lines we are held up
across from one another to each other
over the breathing body of our lives.
Through tightened lips we cry her mercy,
our turbanned lady where she lies,
her violated head shaved, cut, sewn
with tidy stitches over the havoc growth
that is so rich and rank it is not worth
the while of snipping saviors. Their fingers kink
at involuntary failure. She might smile,
now that she's shown her strength.
He tells me that in her last
months at home that is what she did:
she sat in the kitchen rocker and smiled
and chuckled at his effects
at the stove he had set her at
in the front of his mind for years:
she had laughed at his apron strings.
Also, she wrote a letter to her sister in Vancouver,
saying that he was dead.
How her long dimples must have bit into her cheeks!
Then her control went, and she defecated
an afternoon on the bedroom floor
before she slid under and the ambulance was called.
My father told me with some wonder
that when the firemen appeared in her room
with the stretcher, she, on the bed

by that time, smiled.
"Gave them a big smile!" he said. "As though
she was going to a party!" The Fireman's Ball.
What did she want, beyond what any of us
want: money, beauty, power? Why that odd hauteur
when the circumstances of my father's world
waltzed her in reach of them? Their perfume sent
her nostrils cold, she drew
gentility about her like a false
housekeeper's shawl and bowed her head over
ostentatiously simple
invisible embroidery. How she could ply that needle!
They murmured she was hard to know.
Once in a healthy winter when it snowed
she rummaged a square of black
velvet from another of her ages, summoned
me to the open casement window where we leaned
to spread the black patch to catch flakes,
each, she said, perfect, and no two alike,
perfection in the plan and in the execution,
she said, becoming excited with morality
while I saw only changes in the air to earth
the frozen pitch, star-shot
without sound, feather-soft down
from the breast of the owl gray sky
(four o'clock in the afternoon),
plume bristles from the flight of the Arctic fox,
shards of the great icefloe, and ashes
of the fire of sped virtues' light—
I stuck my private tongue out to receive
a flake quick and cool as a wafer
to my topmost earthen root,
but her hair blew in my mouth with the wind,
we were close, her strong
arm rosy with the challenge held
the lovely litter of silence on a shred of night.
How far from earth is air?

vi

That last afternoon, they said, the nurses said,
she would be studying her hand, raising it, so,
against Venetian-blinded light, a not unnatural,
they added, act of those in her condition.
The condition was mortal, of course.
It was not for better or worse,
it was wound with no moral choice, but was mortal chance.
That we were not there was chance, we were in fact
buying an aromatic box
of cigars at the Turks Head Club after late lunch
(we had to feed ourselves with heavy silver).
"I shall never forgive myself." His words.
So she studied: undisturbed
in her special torpor, in a stupor of learning
raised her hand, noted perhaps in her lobotomized
lopsided brain the queer fleshed brace
that let her fingers stretch apart the face
of treacherous air, who smiled and curled
itself instantly unseen
to membrane delicate as moth's
wings between the bones
like thicker twigs but more articulate,
as though trees had her veins.
Her bones could have done anything,
crawl sands, swim, fly,—they will take her far
from where she is, from what they are,
extensions of forgiven time in her they will carry
her out of herself and home
free to her element.
She will go back, but not the way she came.
Did she learn perfection is not bred
by blood but from the bone? Children,
we skip over our dead perpetually
with marrow knowledge of their natural state.
Whose labyrinth is lit

with torches for the speech of worms?
And afterwards the wedding feast.
She must be bride
in name only, escaping through the aperture
of dream she will run hard
through the wood (rivers of waters run
upward, wearing the trunks of trees)
to emerge at the edge of the field and leap
the gate mane flying, constellations
clamoring at her hooves, frightening the birds
who scatter like seeds from her fiery flower
that rides higher, highest, then gulping air
                  like ashes
spins down, rides, glides down
to phoenix rest in a nest of golden sheaves.

All right. But it may not happen like that.
More likely she will suffer,
she
suffered her hand to fall or allowed
it docilely to be put down, yet like
a child towards dark
and we not there
looked towards the door
and waited to be assured
and we not there
to be reassured
before her veins were bubbled out
and the globe of her eye
masked, asked
answer that all is safe, and she is good.

vii

One morning, tourists in the Jeu de Paume,
we checked our umbrellas and swarmed
in damp stockinged feet up slippery stairs
to view the wise old men.

We sliced through Van Gogh and saw
Manet through his model picnic. In a corner, though,
we came on other weather. "Death
of Camille," we peered through steam to read,
stepped back, and there she was,
seen slowly through her veil of snow.
Oh, she came,
ill, beyond old, but ill
the mouth gaped rouged for violets,
the eyelids pressed to themselves browned petals,
the chest crushed antique bouquets.
Sparrows through the eternal whirl of flakes
cried their plucky, desperate *Vite! Vite!*
Dying? She died long ago.
It is the idea of her
that is kept alive through the snow,
as though the young man of the glacier
impeccable in full evening dress
had her fresh with his boutonnière
and they two embraced
in the river of ice
in the mirror of sky
in their glass house roofed with the crystal boughs
of air their victim, jailer, discrete friend.
These lovers—I knew them well—are real.
Do not discount,
either, the plausibility of truth. Mountains move.

viii

It is your absence lies upon these landlocked hills,
the presence of the shadow of a cloud
which like a lowered hand to shadow thought
moves with the train, rests and then passes
with the thought like breath, to catch across a name
at the next unstopped-for station.
A piece of your signpost lodges at my heart,—
to my shame I am ashamed to say that word,

it is suspect, I must have it out,
yet it sticks in my throat: I am ashamed.
I am going home, I suppose, to the West
to leave you I have left before, vacating summer,
asking myself what new things you have sent
ahead to make the lost salt tears rise to my eyes.
It is your absence softens me this time
and lets the hills swim while the rivers swell.
Look, I am going, we are going fast,
we have gathered ourselves, we are leaving behind
what is left of you in our merciless
progress deeper towards the sun. The plain
wears out the hills, the sky grows potent
hourly, we are ripping along the seams
of that quilt
pattern looks so real
you can almost reach out and touch
it, and the pelt
of grass that hides a rage
of insects like small birds (back home
that jay that laughed
blue from a branch of juniper),—
but everything else
is open here, no secrets, barns coffin
new grain (when they lowered you
the jay came out and laughed to the clods
of earth that struck you honestly),
houses boast new roofs.
Farmers walk crops like generals
who stride down ranks of nodding marble
gallused thumbs money dowsers.
Are you the hawk that rides above the yield?
That shadow passes, too. We go,
we have got away, we are moving on,
we have flicked our land-whipping tail past towns
called Nauvoo, Fickle, Antiville,
Kismet, Morocco, Hindustan
the stations no train stops at

no train ever stops at Flytown any more.
We are lengthening out, we are stretching our iron paws
towards the far phalanx, the rocky shields
that bank the sinking fires of the sun.
Almost within our pale single eye we can discern
at the very end of the world
certain small stick-like figures stooping and rising,
stooping and rising, burying day
and raising night in accordance with their task
whose appointer remains nameless by request
but whose beard overflows the peaks at dusk.
One of his eyes, brighter, is larger than the other,
an eagle is a speck of sand in its pupil,
his mouth whistles the whirlwind,
stars jump like fleas in his hair.
It is he whom we must pacify,
it is he who sucks our air
up from our butterfly lungs, thickens our throats
with his fear, sends our limbs sprawling in love
with his darkness, his beating of wings. His beak
caresses the murder of our journey to his light.
You are waiting here.

ix

How shall I blaze noon
being cold and dark as pre-dawn
down to my clay finger-
tips and nails of grayish horn?
No
cock shall crow me up nor the inflamed
and righteous burning
day's eye draw
or mark such mourning for its own.
I want no witness to my will to mine
the black ironic vein wherein I dwell:
I have a purpose now
to raise the grass above that mound

I trespassed in my going.
Yet I know what and where
your house is, what and who
creeps up your stair the while you toss
in your marshy bed amid your sedgey dreams,
and who slinks out before first light, to swing
itself from your backyard tree. I come
by night, by my own night, in stealth, yet bear
my particular phosphorescence.
I am your element, and I ravage,
I scavenge the graves of your worlds.

II

PART TWO

BEYOND THE SUMMERHOUSE

i

Journeys

A scorched leaf
stuck to its window (dirty)
of the slow
moving late departured train

my own head on its own
brain stem turns
stays reading that taut image
struck

on the streaked glass from the one
familiar tree
genus loathing species
loving—I know

those veins that tattered
reflective icon!
After three days
unspeakable conditions

the conductor calls my station
I take my suitcase down
disdain
his black wings his tarnished

medallion show
my documents correctly stamped
To Whom It May Concern
my ticket is continued

Arrivals

No one else
debouches here
this dust-ridden
wind-bitten signboard flapping platform

greets
the empty ticket booth
flutters the clock
stopped at twenty past

the benches bare the floor
even of spit
a school without pupils
who travels this way now

a ghost place
I go out again
to wait and see
that they have sent the trap for me

the pied horse spavined
heavy hoofed not ever
animal I was acquainted with
that patient bony head

nor driver either
hunched yet tall
his glance is sly his nails are long
his coat is borrowed like his grin

No Name is thumbtacked to his back
I do not ask but clamber in
he does not speak but slaps the rein
the horse takes slack and we begin

Journeys

Landscape the flat of a knife
heat rising from
brooding upon that flatness
those reaped fields

that crows drop to
like charred gulls
to feed on culls of grain
under the gape of sky

our road runs straight
no lizard striped rock
no cracked tongued tree
to sing our progress on this plain

only the yellow constant
billow in our wake
hardly horizon save that in the mind
bruised lassitudinous

remembered band beyond
between blue and blue a sail
. . . salt in the eager wound
out of that whirlwind recall

the figure there amid the yield
walking a shade against the glare
pacing the distance alongside of us
where she has walked before

and since in jeopardy of sun
do not walk in the sun
barefoot through stubble
skirt kited up head uncovered

throat open
to the August assault

she must hear our chariot like a hive
our wheels

a thousand thousand bees
humming voices prisoned possibles
to spin her deaf
and rattles by

forget her forgot
she'll be walking centuries in her place
let the birds cry gold
showers of it baubles kisses

high-born lovers dissolving
like the brass green ring
their rainbow wings beat thin
dust in her blazing face

ii

Arrivals

Gates are set wide for us
(I am expected)
the drive narrower than I recall
weeds whisper our swift axle

hedgerows reach out to guide us
into the curve of the circle
the courtyard at last and the clatter
onto the paving stones

grass
spouts from the cracks
the fountain a fist raised dry
before the great cliff of house

—but stop!
He is taking me wrong
the wrong way around
away from the façade

the façade is what I want
orders have been confused
he'll not get my penny
I shall not disembark

amid scratching hens
and the contents of buckets
I know my rights in this matter
I shall enter

through the main portal or not at all
I am practically
a daughter of the estate
I tell you I am expected!

iii

Arrivals

In the pergola
laughter of restitution
a mistake a joke on us
among us nothing has changed

or perhaps change has occurred
but cannot be serious
no one has planned it
nothing is meant by it

a glass of warm tea
the plump girl proffers
her apron smelling of starch
and the clean freshly ironed sea

not far off—
does she have a ploughboy?
The pergola's in shade
a relief

these ordinary kind
faces attentive inquiring

the children's shouts outside
as they romp in the unmown grass

civilization! civilization!
"Our darling . . ."
"So much she's been through . . ."
Gently

he strokes his white silk beard
she amiably croons
both wear light linen
mourning sympathy

rails glitter in my eyes:
"My trunk has it arrived?"
Her pompadour shrugs slightly
jet black she retains

that vanity she spreads
her fine hands ringless
save for the wedding band
where is the ruby that I coveted?

"Dear—you have no idea
you may have to unpack yourself!
Are we finished here?
Just put the glasses on the tray

we'll carry in . . ." Such domestic flurry
he protests: "But the sunset
a most magnificent best of the season
they say—"

"The grass is damp already
call the children do . . . You
incurable then I must though we agreed
it was your responsibility—

Children children . . . time!"
I'll jolly him
tuck his arm under in the old fashion:
"Tell me

is there much honey this year?"
He shakes his white silk head:
"Too much rain in the spring. . . ."
His bones are brittle in their wrinkled sheath

iv

Arrivals

The huge whited shell
inside the same you would think
you could hear the sea in it
the snail growing and retreating

the grizzled wolfhound snarls
from the dry hearth or grins
our same three shadows swell
before us as we climb:

"You'll show me tomorrow?"
"We'll re-acquaint you with the place. . . ."
"That driver?" "Got hold of
a wrong scheme. . . ." I nod we agree

some whip in each of us
in his niche the blackamoor
hoists his dead torch
the lamp unlit hangs on its chain

her skirts a skein of sound
voice a silk winding: "But for tonight
for tonight she must rest. . . ." A chime
oh do not let me dream

i

Soundings

I meet her on the terrace facing West
she too is combed and dressed
for the duel
we sit at the glass-topped table

her wrist pouring out stops lies:
"You slept I trust you slept
well?" The cup and her concern
I can thank her for those

he is approaching below
by a vegetable walk
his skylight gaze catches us
jauntily

he waves his stick: "A moment!
Mark me as I progress
save me a crumb!"
She murmurs: "You would never guess. . . ."

"What?" "He takes it seriously. . . ."
"What?" "He will say it is
a fox in the chicken run
a rat in the granary

a poacher in the wood
a thief in the orchard—pah!
Mere crutches! Lies . . ."
"But why?" She shrugs: "Fear . . ."

"Of what?" "Judgement—
of poverty which is death—
maybe of paradise . . ."
"But this is paradise!"

I falter how she pursues:
"You say that for you see it
as it was you years ago
on holiday you are not

what you were we are not. . . ."
"The children they don't change—"
"You've noticed? you're quite right
they're in a different scheme. . . .

Oh I could show you more
things you ought to have seen
before now and now
you will have to find

yourself paradise and hell
the snake with its tail tongued to its mouth
rolling downhill—
I know enough of both!"

"And where does limbo come?"
A blind falls shut on that
no further word
from that quarter

"Here we are here we are!
Prepared are we for our stroll?
We're promised each to each?"
So droll today he seizes

her cup and drains it: "We're off. . . ."
"Wait—the children
where have they got to what
are they playing at?"

"Nests
of nettles I daresay haha!
Poor little beggars in the summerhouse . . .
My dear?"

iii

Journeys

So we set out on foot
how far from yesterday
we travel not true North
the needle's quivering tip

on the mental map but a limping
compass circumscribed

subject to
his game limb (a shooting accident)

diminishing returns
burned barns and pilfered bins
drought or flood
always at wrong junctures so the kine

drop their young stillborn
crops decay in the leaf
at midnight horses go lame
arbors wizen at noon

shamed articles to grief
I listen as I am meant
trail his hooded whimsical
track with its bitter

trivial sincere travail
nothing brave about it
a sort of crippled bravado seeking sidewise
approval of apologies

his voice sawing on like the caw
of a crow telling blackened beads
he would overwhelm my history with his failure
I allow it him freely

but at the chapel bell
at an hour of my choosing
he shall do penance
he shall kneel and I shall pray

ii

Soundings

Elsewhere in early afternoon
(my foiled priest has gone in
to rooms she continually
exits from)

I am spying
my roots like willow
my branches in disguise
the childish stream of prattle

enters my leaves: "Your name
what is your name today?"
"My name today is Ben. . . ."
Amused: "What does Ben do

today?"
"Fetches stick and growls!"
And to the other the same:
"What is your name today?"

"My name is Bet I am the doll—"
"Ben must take Bet
by the throat and shake her so—"
"To hurt her?" "Just a bit . . .

She must get down and beg
for mercy . . . Oh
well done!" A slight clapping
as at chamber music

and then the snap of steel:
"What is my name forever?"
Syllables on the stream
sighing the ripples of:

"Lilla . . . Lilla . . ." I lean close
through my foliage Lilla it is
unchanged my favorite
in charge

charming in white
eyelet and hazel switch
the pupil stitched black through the iris:
"Lilla tell us

why we are not allowed
to wander why they snatch us back

from the wall and the gate
the hedgerows miss us and the shore—"

What can my favorite say?
She takes a breath begins her lie:
"A guest is here who does not know
she is the cause of our disease

we seem the same as when we were
she does not tally us as ghosts
nor realize she is one of us
she catches only glimpses of—"

"What shall we do to her?"
"What does she want of us?"
"She wants us live
my dears she wants us where

she taught us how the world was round
and empire red she wants
things simple she wants things polite. . . ."
"What shall her name be soon?"

All my leaves tremble at her smile:
"She'll dowse for it with the wand
she'll walk the estate over
with her dainty shoes!

After exploring of the cave
after the fire on the shore
(we'll wrap her in green leaves
a poultice to her scars)

when she has learned
or when she has been taught
we may give her a clue . . ."
"What can we do besides?"

"Pray the fine weather holds
play tricks in biding time
and promise to be true. . . .
She shall be satisfied!"

Arrivals

Tea-time and the doctor the one
official the other not
riding his sorrel at an easy trot
up the drive his soft

fedora dropped across his suede
vested interest
pince-nez informality that goatee
hhm hhm: "I find you as I imagined

assembled in the belvedere
the family plot
my joke you're looking uncommonly
. . . . since you insist—"

She calls out at once:
"Maizie! We want another setting. . . ."
Flashing with laughter:
"What would you suggest?"

"My treatment seems to be working!"
"Delightful you recall
our guest of long ago
she was no older than—

here's the girl now. . . ."
He bows cool as a knife
at our meeting how he is deft
how he squinted:

"Hot water quick!
These servants these days . . ."
She's right I could have done better
I shall remain demure

watching her fan-like hands
hover

white doves among the tumblers
I am of course wearing black in my position:

"I fear I am putting you out
shutting my surgery for the hour
wanting speech with coevals. . . ."
He pinches his nose: "Weary work

mine bumpkins
pitchforks grindstones scythes
kerosene childbirths by lamplight—
ah that's delicious!"

He wipes his neat moustache
sets his glass down with a thump
like a blunt instrument on a kitchen table:
"Where are my godchildren hiding?"

"Planning tomorrow's picnic I daresay
you'll come? You'll be wanted certainly!"
"Count on me. . . ." His fingers drum
he hums a tune his nails have grown

iii

Soundings

Next day however rains
the gardens fume
from my blurred window
trees droop with damp

the summerhouse assumes
a Chinese attitude
indoors the dog whines and yawns
he naps and she winds yarn

nothing to do but explore
search rooms try locks
what a large house this is!
How many portraits of the dead

passed over by the brush of time

so much yearning furniture
shrouded in dustsheets and regrets
a queer bourne this hush!

Soundless up the attic treads
crouch
ear to the panel thumb to the latch—
if I should catch them

at their mischief of
boxes and trunks in exile
Lilla parading in my shawl
the boy in my tartan the girl in my sash

my henna wig mismated—
by the keyhole my eye fits
only Lilla reading to
them clustered at her plaided knee

they listen like birds:
"'So then
they flew over oceans and islands
over lakes and woods and the cold

wind whistled where wolves howled. . . .'"
Angelic
we are all enchanted: "'The black crows
flew screaming. . . .'" Charred

gulls under the gape of sky
under transparencies of circumstance
I grope the stair beside the twisted rope
someone should light that lamp

i

Viewings

Amid anonymous monocles
perambulating
young ladies in waists and villas
we are preserved

perceived in wicker chairs
"At the Summer Residence"
in gazebo ease
"North of" after croquet

(a mallet tilts across his knees)
how genteel
the doctor clicked
she said and kissed me

we must take care he agreed
the wolfhound grinned—
I would have
buried it under three stones

but they persuaded
how we must think of the future
the children have not changed
where the light falls

the temple retains that fatal hollow
their eyes do not reflect
except the sky's pale gift
they are thieves too

twine their art
about you like the nightshade vine
the cold wind could whistle
they would assert its warmth

they could cut you to the bone
meaning no harm truly
you could sicken and die
courting disaster and applause

I am trying
to see myself clearly in the group
surely
I am there in the corner

of the camera's report
my black dress shows plainly

yet at the explosion
I must have flinched

or the photographer
bungled I have no features I appear
to be leaning forward
warning or seeking to warn

i

Fêtes

The day appointed and the laden breeze
draws up live voices at the dawn
scatters the ashes in the grate
the soft occasional

fumbling on shingle of the tide
filling the far rock pools
recovers resonance and wrack
and on the mantelpiece the row of shells

cowrie and mitre
moon snail and virgin nerites
echoes
remnants of naming of things—

Weltschmerz au revoir
baskets are being packed
cloaks and staffs called for
also parasols

everyone drinking coffee standing up
the children darting and quarrelling
everywhere everything in a word
normal on schedule here's the tumbrel

we scramble in with our baggage
Maizie has plucked a rose
for our driver blushing he starts
we are hurled backward what a flourish

what a spectacle! Hens scuttle

the dog howls
us down the lane and out the gates
as though he knows our fates

as though we are not already
having negotiated the turn singing
he beating time with his stick
she thrumming alto cicada

Lilla
bawls like a little drunk
in my ear the children shriek
impossible to keep the tune

the driver's shoulders heave
he's in disguise it's obvious
a mile away
we're whirling by

the figure walking
fold on fold the field
alongside the smoking road
she has moved up on us

stalking
extending her hold
sighting us vigil wise against the wind—
dust in her blazing face

ii

Fêtes

The end of the road to the sea
at the sea the end of the land
the low bluff promontory
the tip

leading into
earth into water and the airy waves
the skirmish to halt
halloo!

Hats off!
The doctor leaps down brandishing
shouting we slide to surround him
we knew it a success

he rang the bell with us
a merry scene
the ancient concertina
the horse's girth

wheezes accompaniment
to our unloading impedimenta
impatient the sea gavottes
the tide is high

the water blue dazzle
shall we be able to bathe
to perform our ablutions
for the once we plead

the duty of pleasure we can feel
already the plunge the splash
our skin tingles imagining
that impact while she poses

apart withdrawn
white under white umbrella
and the paternal or avuncular
frown

advises first things first
the driftwood if we want the fire
we want the fire
must be hauled

impaled
log tree root and spar
towards darkness the bonfire will show best
against darkness

they will be able to see it for miles
from their black ships or flickering

cottage windows
so he chuckles

settles his chin on his stick to supervise
this gathering in his hectare
and we fetch
lumber under the sun:

"Is it ready yet?"
"It is taller than we are!"
Oh he would have it to heaven
if it were left to him

but the doctor splendid in shirtsleeves
heaves the last log into place
his eyeglass ribbon ripples
he clashes his palms together

the hairs on his arms golden wires
she strolls through filtered light
over bone-white pebbles
she swishes towards him: "So?"

"Finished for what it is worth!
A monument to be consumed. . . ."
"Monuments
should be consumed. . . ." Superb

she starts to turn away
he parodies a bow they do not touch:
"Shall we swim then now?"
"You may—I've done with such. . . ."

This time she does
fierce and indifferent turn
bereft
he shrugs and hollows his bright hands

about his red lips and bellows
released
flinging off we arrow to reward—bemused
the crow on the fencepost watches

Fêtes

Half-clothed in this loud embrace
trammeled boisterous by the shock
of the element we tumble
we shout in the welter

they swim like eels
teasing winnowing the water
or like finny creatures nipping
at weeds and thighs

their slight wet teeth
they lure me out from the shallows
I flailing when I go under
his arms bring me up

gasping I am briny
my hair gushes over his wrists
the sun glows like kerosene
the clouds blister like steam

they surface
laughing they treadle
the buoyancy Lilla lays
a kelp frond on my breast

they help me staggering to shore
their bodies glisten with salt
lithe as though newly arisen
they prop me against the pyre:

"Mademoiselle—" "Good girl—"
As though it happens every day with him
("'Weary work mine'")
they race back to their element

their games
she approaches slowly with her basket

having furled her parasol
and struck it between two stones

from another direction
he also limping they converge
saying simply and offering
nourishment that we must

after such experience accept
I am asked to trust
a piece of bread a glass of wine
let the others sport

let them dally in the surf
we shall assent they imply
to the shale's hard comfort and confer
concerning our identical impotence

i

The Cave

Echo echo *ecce*
wrenched and infinitely injured
voices ricochet
from shelves and corners mock

and hoot mimick
birds at aurorean carol
animals at dusk
snufflings (if we have met walls

fingers come wet away) and human
susurrations
in the interstices
hum

silence
the silence
the silence runs
like water in the dark

over the rock of itself
within this rough dome of this dark
I stumble
something is thrust

at me instantly he lends
he is lending
bending towards me in the avocal silence
he lendeth me

his stick
which I strike
against a stalactite like a bell
hollow the knell redounds

from that inverted steeple
bleak and deep the toll
recoil
fooled foiled again I reel

from behind that perverted pillar
Lilla's laugh rings out
soft
peal upon peal—

I must stand out against
keep my wits remember
that I am practically
remember my justifying vow and my possession

now of the taproot therefore of the tree
that wraps the cave in its talons
up there
in that other cave

innameable immanent
I shall retain what he gave me
in the name of
in the name of

Fêtes

We struggle out
half-blinded blinking and ragged
tattered at nerves' ends
under the jangling rays

In this din this radiance
against what must happen
what has happened already elsewhere
in the world—

I mean the dying of the day:
"We must prepare!"
Her hurly-burly
so she will clap us

will she
into good spirits will she
beguile us would she dare
project on this shore's scrim

enacted scenes
of innocence and joy innocent
because of joy earnest
because of innocence

she cannot gain our gaze
our gaze does not reflect
it is waiting for the fire
to fasten upon the fire

our ears cannot hear
being already attuned
to the attenuated crackling of the air
such words as she might have spoken

such music she might have made
dry like foam on her lips

within the sullen hour
halt

would I help if I could
("'So much she's been through'")
the children fret and chafe
Lilla draws them with her

foresighted
she has brought a toy
she has hidden among the rocks
she shows them

I would have shown them
leaning forward warning
or seeking to warn
my black dress billowing a black sail

on this stony ground
with my stick I would have
I would have tried to trace with my stick
the first letter of their alphabet

i

The Fire

A zone of dusk
the purple thickens the sea
the wind has subsided:
"Soon? Is it to be soon?"

"Very soon now . . . watch for the star
the one particular star
that wheels into position
there at the mid-horizon. . . ."

"Will the moon come too?"
"I if I were you
would not count on the moon. . . ."
Far out the sea shivers silver

as though someone has lit
a single lamp in the darkened cave of the air

a lantern in a ruined barn at night
a flare on a rustic table it blooms out

the pile looms behind us
anticipatory
we have crept
from our various shelters

to stand before to stare
at the soft refulgence
presently many stars
glitter less faintly

who will strike the match
our counterpart
limping and wincing he lofts
the small box

he carries the coffin of little lights
marries
the tinder to the flame
shifts it tenderly

ceremonious
into the heart of our driftwood
furnace that catches
instantly what colors

it is the salt rose ochre
the speech of blue tongues
leaping
from log to log consuming

a dance dance dance
savages stamp
high haigh haigh higher
oh we would have it to heaven

our arms beseech like branches
our feet beat upon the stones like metal
sparks fly from our ignited eyes
as the fire mounts we break

off to dance on our own
we whirl glowing we burn with the element
molten our veins our vitals tremulous
(only her leaf is white)—

the children's mouths open as they tread
buoyant and lambent in the noise
in the roiling welter
possessed

I throw my stick in like a crutch
to be blessed it is spun right up
a feathered spear a straw
in the roaring of timbers

he hops towards me
his arms outstretched
the heat lifts his hair like ash
our arms beseech each other like branches

ii

The Fire

Lilla dancing stumbles
the doll the wax object
hurtles from her grasp into
that inferno her face blazes

I rush I shall rescue
my favorite
I put my hand in
snatch what is hers

what doll what mask what pain
it is nothing but my own
I cower I cover my features
the dripping wax from my fingers

blisters
my face hardens grows older
instant by instant I have known it

but in no mirror of mine

I have pain to endure
the doctor works nimbly: "You will seem
yourself in no time. . . .
There will be no scars. . . . *Calme-toi!*"

So: I am being taken care of—
but what is my name
what is my name forever?
What nervous wind stirs in the embers?

i

Departures

By the red artifice of coals
the picnic is over
she collects her parasol
the children have their souvenirs

I am retiring in disgrace
her skirt says without a word
he disagrees I nod we agree
then we have made that peace

together we meet at land's end
the hooded ferryman
hired to oar us home
around the nightbound coast

below the cliff wings cut
suspect shapes
hover crying of oceans and islands
over our heads

at the cliff's top a private fire
like anxious tropic birds
in a strange climate flits
in a cage of shadows a figure

devotional
as our craft

slips so far beneath her
dividing the spineless waves

a brand in a long arc falls
hissing across our bow
the boatman veers—a momentary
phosphorescence—

his shoulders indicate
no more than that
(I cannot read
the placard on his back)

a burning bone dazzled out
the children huddle sleepily
clasping their treasures
she sits upright

as on a bench the boat is bearing
across the dark lawn he mumbles:
"No further word from that quarter. . . ."
She: "What did you expect?"

vi

Arrivals

At the dock he pays the boatman off
(I never saw his face
but his eyes gleamed like a slave's
behind the black bandage—

he bit each coin):
"Until next time!" Under night's blanketing
the lightly jarring sound
of retreating oars: "Next time!"

"Children children . . . Lilla
look after the little ones do
they stagger on the path
how they are weighted with stones!"

She is sullen scarcely more
than a child herself when I return

I shall make sure to send to her
a gift of some value to atone

for the loss of her plaything
a book would be most instructive
the book russet-bound with pages
the color of wasps' nests and waterstained

on the fly-leaf
written in spider's drift she will find
intertwined our names a nice conceit
she will be disappointed

vii

Arrivals

This country has no moon
but the birch trees we go between
glimmer weakly like photographs
of dressed women of another siècle

among them we pick diffidently
our way not talking
as in a museum of the future
we do not credit these trees

how smoothly she moves
propels us out of the woods
onto the sweet grass before the summerhouse
the doctor lounges puffing his cigar:

"I got back early by moonlight
the horse stepped right along. . . ."
The rose in his buttonhole
blooms black in the bud

Maizie emerges blushing
her apron smells fresh she smiles
takes his arm in the new way
she frowns and we go on

towards the house the huge
whited shell

lit up as for a festival
we press on towards the façade

Fêtes

The fountain plays such tunes!
Village musicians
scrape and blow
crickets and staghorn beetles on the terrace

from the plump balcony the mayor
regales us in patois following the speech
such a spurt
the moss is annihilated

carp raise their heads in the basin
in the courtyard
they are singing in stanzas
heavy boots clump the rhythmic pavement

the dog wildly barks waltzing
I receive many compliments
a drunken peasant bestows the prize
a chaplet of milkweed pods

it is exhilarating
being at one with the crowd
beneath its uniform exterior
my marble face might have veins

the blood might beat in my encapsulated brow
like little gongs in a village church
quick quick quick quick
the candles chant in my kindled eyes

ii

Départures

Cockcrow
cockcrow

PART TWO | 87

cockcrow
once twice thrice from the unseen dunghill

at the first crow of the cock
the violins shy like frightened horses
the drum clots suddenly
a crack appears in the main portico

at the second crow of the cock
"A storm?" she queries swaying past
in the exalted mayor's arms
at the third crow of the cock

the dancers scatter like rinds
before the whirlwind
carriages pelt headlong
down the avenue lanterns gibbering

passengers striving to fasten the curtains
at each other's throats
in the confusion
in the convulsion

the carp are extinguished
the fountain swallows itself
insensible
the mayor sprawls in a ditch

she has twitched her robe about her
fled indoors I pursue—
the blackamoor
hoists his dead torch

that lamp is almost out
his body dwindling from the twisted rope
could I arouse this household
she is there above me

bald as a darning egg
toothless and hunched
at her empty safe
unhinged—

"Thieves have got in. . . ."
Where is the ruby that I coveted?
"My treasures! My treasures!"
My heart's chamber pulses red

iii

Departures

Mist
rises like incense from the hedgerows
into the burning field of morning
the furrowed road

spills dust from my heels like pollen
my road runs straight
no figure paces mine
my shadow is my own

no sentinel
marks my progress
barefoot through stubble
daring to walk in the sun

skirt kited up head uncovered
throat bare to the august assault
such journeys always
end in leave-taking

iv

Departures

On the platform the doctor stammers
of luggage and traps
("The horse stepped right along")
I interrupt:

"You wish to wish me well?
I thank you for the charity. . . ."
I can afford these trifles now:
"And she?"

"Will be walking centuries in her place. . . ."
"No pity?" "None!" "The children?"
"None . . . No—none!"
Rails glitter in my eyes:

"No harm
no harm was meant I swear—" I swear
they could cut you to the bone
meaning no harm truly:

"How the wind blows out here
enough to dry your marrow!"
Grit between my teeth
I mount the iron steps

present him my countenance
pitiful he is so changed
I enter the narrow cage
and the iron door clangs to

iv

Journeys

To Whom It May Concern:
We are inching South
like the black finger of a glacier
under unspeakable conditions

food is thrust at us through windows
some have fought over water
there are rumors of pox
still one must persevere

I too have erred I confess it
between times I doze
nod off
dreaming of children and a summerhouse

this heat is stifling
heat lifts my hair into ash
I stretch my arms towards them beseeching
crying out into their dreams

"Civilization! Civilization!"
A scorched leaf
tattered
reflective icon

I thought you were real my darlings
you were only the shadows of my eyes
that opened once fitfully
widened in fear and suspicion

and closed again like flowers
blank as that sky before snow
meanwhile
my head on its brain stem turns

stays reading
my documents in order
farewell farewell
I shall write from Genoa

already I hear the sea wind
slapping the sails towards the new world
the gulls
circle high in the bright blue cave

POEM OVERHEARD
IN A MAINE DOCTOR'S WAITING ROOM

"I never go out in weather like this
I never go out in weather like this
I was married on the shortest day
of the year fifty years ago and that's why
I've never forgotten it
my great-great grandmother married when she
was sixteen two families pioneered
pioneers in Limestone
I get so cold at night
my bones ache and I can't move so I come here
and the doctor gives me something
they had no shelter for the only cow in Limestone
that first night so the young bride flew out
from the covered wagon and pegged a quilt
a brand-new wedding gift around the cow
during the night it snowed
and in the morning when they went out
they saw the steam
coming from under the edges of the blanket
the bride was milkmaid and that very day
the young lads and the bridegroom
built the shelter"

NIGHTWALK

"This lassitude,
this filthy languor,
this inability to laugh or weep or to decide
not to decide—
going on now for weeks of weather
inward, bland,
neither ennui nor anomie,
neither honest snow nor cheating rain
but cloudy, heavy, gray of gray,
the wearing on of day to unaccomplished day,
a kind of mononucleosis of the will.

"So last night, not unsleeping yet not yet asleep,
I got up out of what I had assumed
a bed humanly warmed, and crept in dark
downstairs, Lady Macbeth of Main Street,
the Bovary of the block.
The household
breathed deep and innocent around—
why should it not? These dreamers are real,
at least they dream real dreams. Outside,
it snows. The real glass paperweight
is gently shaken of the world.

"I know each step here, where the creaks are,
I know each passage through each room,
I have made this household, these rooms
these children and their dreams, and him
and his, mine. Out of myself. Now I am hungry,
not for food, but for what might be mine

only. What greed,
in a place where children die of hunger.

"I open, delicate, diffident, novice to this greed,
the wide white door.
The little bulb blooms like an icicle.
Such stuff
we fill ourselves with! Plastic cheese, pizzas,
store bread, lettuce like counterfeit
money, hard fruit, something called
Grandma's Warm-Up Blueberry Turnovers—
and, of course, milk. From cows, we may presume.
Milk first, then. What we've had drummed earliest
into our infant bellies. It tastes smooth, and cold,
we have grown used to the coldness of milk, we
have made it a virtue, the smoothness of cold
whiteness in the childish cup. So,
emptied of thought, so
easily satisfied, I lick off my mustache.

"The door gapes all this time, the bill will rise
with this midnight feasting . . .
In clear as false air wrapping, like a new
fashion for some emperor's friends in vogue
a pound of hamburger
packed like solid measles. I pick it up, disinter
it, weigh it in my hand as an intern might
a brain disengaged. But cannot wait
and ravenous break the transparent membrane with my teeth,
spit the wrapping out, take the chunk of raw
meat into my jaws, and chew. Salt,
salt, it needs salt, and my eyes
are doing that at last, the liquid runs
down onto the meat. It's true, it's true,
the flavor is improved by tears.

"In the crooked rocker the cat sleeps
and never stirs to welcome me to his professional

community. His black-and-white
plush covers an earlier nocturne.
My mouse, my weasel I had to buy
to savage it again. Even its red
color is injected, I understand, but I understand
it is what I make do with.
The rawness and the salt are perhaps
a beginning.
And my zestful teeth are sharp.

"Strength, strength,
and newness in the blood.
Close the door softly on the light
and sneak,
a walking owl, up to my nest.
My eyes grow big in dark. The snow
still falling keeps my kingdom fresh.
My beak
parts in a killing smile, and salt like sweet
sand rests on my rasping tongue. In the morning
they will say how well I must have slept."

LIVES OF THE POET

i

The poet lets the cat
out
by the ordinary
door

ii

The owl is the only bird who
reminds me of a cat
it is the eye
like a single agate
cut in two
by a frugal crafter

iii

It was not the fault of the gnat
that he flew
onto my eyeball
as I
was gazing at the Parthenon

iv

Down at the cove
of the seven sycamores
even the fish are singing
because the girl
in the red dress
is coming

v

My friend said Mirrors
don't wear out you can
look into one for years
and it shows no change
think of that
she said I did

vi

So much rain this summer
even the fleas
have become dispirited

vii

Toad
like a hackberry leaf
under the mulberry tree

viii

Half of the berry tree is dead
the other half has never borne
so heavily
I could almost believe
it speaks to me

ix

Hear the crows'
black
barking in the wood

x

Suddenly the Chinese elm
sheds its dark
crown of birds

xi

The heel of my shoe
squeaks like a cricket
across the stone floors
of the autumn

xii

On the side lawn
sweating in the spring
the poet kneeling
grubs the teeth of lions

THIS PERSON

This person that I knew changed her dress
every afternoon at four o'clock,
having washed her private parts
in the black-and-white
tiled genteel bathroom
and put perfume on of a pale floral scent,
to sit on the back porch swing under the green-
and-white awning to wait,
clean hands in fresh lap,
for only she knew what.
For years and years she did that,

and it was only my father who drove in
in the Studebaker, later the Buick, never
a Cadillac, which would have been
ostentatious, but his father
would have loved it, not being suburban,
simply a big frog
in a village puddle: him with his cupola
and his columns and his bonhomie,
his binoculars to watch the big boats
in the channel—I sometimes thought
it was him she waited for, in a queer fashion
during visits, they got on.

He might have understood, supported
what the other, darker and more nervous,
had cut off at the root. Inverse snobbery.
We are better, so we live worse. And she,
remembering cutwork and chromos and raspberries
floating in cream, not realizing country

power, came innocent to everything.
Stopped reading, music, tried the cards,
dressed dolls, sawdust tarts that sprawled on beds
for charity, and in three days had a child
that would ride a tricycle full tilt
into the special wallpaper of the claustrophobia.

Married, I escaped, yet I would pace
my guilt with my children across half a continent
to wheel onto the neglected gravel at five o'clock
precisely (twelve hours from Painesville)
beside the thin hibiscus—they never would give
that tropical bloom: thrown-up peanuts
on the back seat, crayons everywhere, and the recent
headache from tunnels on the Pike and vapor lock,
and the thousands of paper napkins and happy stories:
there she would be,

sitting in the swing, waiting,
and he, of course, late at the office.

Oh, she could be awful. Made the son
sit in a straight chair when he did not want to,
"An exercise in discipline," looked at a drawing
of a covered wagon and two horses (I knew), sneered,
"Is that the best you can do?"
I could have killed her then; but when the two
were old enough to learn dominoes and she taught
them at the kitchen table but kept pushing
the black-and-white tabs into perfect place, I decided
There's no earthly use. In fact, they enjoyed it.

I woke suddenly.
Silent as she stepped (the attic door, for she slept
up there now, left open for the flow of air)
and purposeful as silence, I awoke, heart
alert and eyes, my pupils, staring, listening.
The little girl

slept in the cot next my bed. She came and lowered,
a dim shape in her modest nightgown, over the cot.
She could have had a razor, or removed,
so gently, the mortal pillow from under the small head.
I saw the two figures, one bodily
echo of my own, and the other, bending.
No need to think of breathing.
What she did
was to lift a single strand
of limp warm hair from that head, take it into her hand
and stroke it so lightly that a bird
would not wake.
I heard the sigh, piteous, pitying,
and the dawn-wind words: "Ah, the pretty,
oh, the poor pretty thing."
I could have loved her, then,
had I not been coward there, and since.
Pretty. Poor pretty thing.

Time, and times. And my tall, now,
for her age
daughter says, as I come down
another staircase
from another day's
stress as from a wooden platform
erected permanently behind the eyes of my mind,
"I like the way you always change
your dress before supper"; I don't wince
unless it is to smile; and we both watch
for the car turning in to the drive.

THE OLD HOUSE

Ivy swings inward at the window,
Three wasps crawl upon the pane,
Elderly wasps and older ivy.
Ivy is fancy, wasps are plain.

Here lived the beautiful Hotchkiss sisters:
Laura, Eulalia, and Emily Jane.
Once they were courted by half the county
(Ivy is fancy, wasps are plain).

Once they were courted by half the county,
carriages thronging the riverbent lane,
Tall young men with presents and prospects
(Three wasps buzz upon the pane).

Father remarked of the frequent proposals
To Laura, Eulalia, and Emily Jane
(Father was rich and Mama was poorly),
"Somebody's loss is somebody's gain."

(Ivy swings inward at the window.)
Daughters are daughters, and love is vain.
Here live the elderly Hotchkiss sisters.
Three wasps buzz upon the pane.

THE LOST BOY

His photograph got in
with the family others. Nobody recognizes
him, not even the everybody's mother.
S. T. Wiggins, Ground Floor Gallery, No. 15
Commercial Street, Cedar Rapids, Iowa
is what's printed on
the back of the evidence.
Oh, the careful combing of his hair!
Two years old probably, he retains
his Buddha look, inscrutable, hinting at worlds.
Exquisite listening ear,
adze nose, his mouth judgemental, remarkable
in one so young; in a dress and sash.
A single booted foot protrudes beneath the hem.
Its angle I could kiss with reverence.
The fingers of the tiny hands dispose
themselves politically upon the fierce
upholstered arms of the chair that suffers
them, ending in tired lion's claws.
He has a power.
More than statesman, not much less
than transplanted god,
such a passenger
sits, a good baby, for the lens.
I should say before the First World War.
I told you, worlds ago. He does not whimper
or dwindle. He has disappeared from our mirrors
that he might have inherited: no,
he comes because he is gone,
having chosen perhaps to go with that clear
intimidating gaze,

to lisp at Plato's knees, from Emerson
and Thoreau, Hawthorne among the sycamores.
Hedges of Osage oranges
stand between him and them. Nevertheless,
Negatives available for future orders.

DISJUNCTIVE

Your days go more quickly than ours.
Here in the 3 a.m. dark
we grow restless because of the daylight
greeting of doves in your dooryard.
The clink of your breakfast spoons
as they round the teacups disturbs us,
also the brightness of the marmalade.
When we rise rumpled from bed
you have already gone on the river,
one of you leisurely poling the punt,
the other, the Cornish-haired girl,
trailing her hand in the water.
As the warmth recedes from the meadows
and a late thrush sings in the wood,
noon strides into our field.
At our supper, you fall asleep.
Our midnights don't mingle, our dreams
hang separate as planets.
When you touch down again on our tarmac
our meeting will turn back,
turn forward the intimate clock.

MEMENTO

Aunt Eva came that year across the lake
from Toronto on the steamer: she was big,
full-breasted, almost six feet tall.
She wore a blue suit and a white crepe blouse
with a jabot. She was coming home.

Dark, bulky, imperious
with the family charm, she brought legends:
singing in her sleep after voice lessons,
divorce, the second-floor suicide door
she nearly walked out of—she brought me
a necklace of forget-me-nots,

blue and white small beads
knotted tightly with no space between.
"Here we are," she said, resonant, clasping
her gift round my nine-year-old neck.
I never knew why, then, there, so immediate
with the car waiting.
The back of the steamer was churning.

Next summer she was down
to a skeleton. One Sunday morning
in her red bathrobe in the Port house
as I was playing Grieg's "Butterfly" on the upright,
she leaned on the parlor door-frame
her hand a yellow leaf on the polished wood.
When I had finished, she said from a hollow,
"Don't let them stop you. Don't forget."

FOR FRIENDS, ON THE BIRTH OF REBECCA

Make all you can of beauty quickly.
The rush in the blood, the heightening
blush to the cheek of the lovely—
take measure of these, and advantage:
look at topography and time in this new face,
remark indent of valley, sweet dusky swell
of hills above milky lakes
(morning mist). Do not dwell
on vacancies of this landscape
but imagine a music for reeds, music toneless and lunar;
before it fades, recall the radiance of
other geographies in other spheres.
If you must turn away at last,
gaze deep here first at least.

SUBSISTENCE LEVEL

It is in a marginal land that subsistence is possible.
Find me water, bring it in your hands,
expect some spilling and go back
a thousand times to the fortunate spring:
I've selected
pebbles and grasses for the soup.
Now make me fire, rub and rub,
I'll breathe and we'll be warm.
Thankful for remnants, stones, weeds, breath.
Contaminated as they are!
                              The satellites
are bright tonight. Although I miss the stars
the bloody sun will rise with its familiar dust
at what we are accustomed to call dawn.

It is in a marginal land
one reads the old book of the mind,
the pages stained, the print blurred,
the title torn away and the spine bitten,
slurring the evidence fitfully yet stubborn
with irritation at the lapses
of memory, the withering of cells.
Twig for pencil, one marks for a while
certain phrases that have a turn;
and when the twig wears out, the fingernail
grows with a life of its own.
Love. Not fair. And, where did we go wrong?
We are left with our bodies and our will,
and the sky which, after the firestorm, may fail.

After the grass, the roots. The dirt last.
If you die,

I have no shovel.
                    Condors, take care.
You see I know your name. You have an enemy below
before my eyes become clear glass
through which reflections and their objects pass
without trace, filtered by liquid and by air
till eyes and objects disappear
along with our picked bones
(the flesh consumed since that we called
beautiful, and we were right). Care, take care,
'A stone look on a stone's face.'
Yet when my love comes walking
towards me on his ghostly sticks
I shall recognize his insect guise,

his gaze like staring lozenges
bent upon wires, and his elegant, imploring glance,
I shall leave off eating earth and raise
myself on the widow of an elbow,
feel it resolve, absolved to wing
like cloud, veined, and sized
to match his own. My abdomen folds in,
I put out legs for extra antennae, my vision's
cut to facets, my brain shrinks
to the head of a pin. Even though the sun
remain poised a moment more before the final plunge,
we shall have cast off for the flight
and, coupled, indissoluble, entered the world.
At sunset, the wind dropped, and it was possible
to begin to assess the extent of the destruction.

OBJECTS OF VISION

I

I am in the mirror
my image is in the mirror
my two eyes thus
my nose my mouth I imagine
my image in the mirror
except for the mark the blemish
where I have placed
my finger on my lips

hush! my mind is in the dark
conspiring
at the back of the silver
listening waiting
as though behind a window shutter
for the crowds that pass in the street
for the one figure to detach itself
and come forward to the glass

II

In the country of the tree
the single leaf that falls
is of course the tree
falling from itself

and the stone already lichened
in the field of the tree
the hieroglyph of the leaf
can change the meaning of

III

Leaning over the edge
looking down into the well
one sees an eye
magnified by water
surrounded by stone
one's eye reflected
a welling of darkness
one could drown in that eye

IV

A leaf fallen and floating
on the surface of the water
a note on a mirror
an idea from outside

V

On the stone fronts of the many houses
the damp has made vital impressions
as of hands of the blind
feeling their way to the market
to the bazaars
most of the windows are shuttered
behind them one senses an eye
appliquéd to the blind
waiting for the refraction
of light on the oblique
in the darkness of living rooms
the white caps of housewives quiver
the tree-patterned paper puts down roots
the grandfather taps with his cane
as he climbs the stair to the attic
where at night the moon shines in
he crosses on his way

to the window and the telescope
the moon tonight is full he hunches to
she leaps to his watery eye
beset with stars in his dotage
in his excitement he reads
the cloud passing over her countenance
as a letter from a rival
an idea from outside

VI

An old man with his eye pressed to an image within
a brain overgrown with patterns like a stone in
                 a field
an aged grasshopper in a green frock coat
an old opera-goer
(having hung up his cloak and cane)
still I am drawn to him
his gaze on my craters
his daughter endures him
his son-in-law despises him
if a child laughs he weeps
for the end of laughter
for him I could preen shall become
all round and silver forthwith for this miser
hoarder of my sensational coin
how he would lie about me how he would like
to slide me under his mattress
take me out polish me during his daily siesta
his windfall his dearest
put me a monocle to his memories
I slide away from his lens up the sky
an idea an image he a cloud
passing over my countenance
a mote on a mirror
a leaf on the surface
changing the meaning of

III

PART THREE

A DAY AT THE SHORE

amicitia: early morning   all the time in the world
not a cloud in the sky   we exclaim   trailing our paraphernalia
striped towels caftans totes Ozymandian chairs
we come over the rise   of the dunes through the spears
of the pale   beach grass to the wind-   stippled sands of the
      reach
and loll of ocean   that greenswell   high swirl and foam blithe
I follow Virgil   arbiter of place   we settle our effects
among other worshipers   in ritual anoint   our city flesh
all the same   temporary tenants   of the colloquial echolalia
egos in Arcady circadian   gulls of the outermost circle
each of us   Virgil says   with only   so many stories to tell
of a length prescribed but endless   put into air   like this

fair island's breath   the long salt hollow rush   sustains
the great carp rippling kite   white-and-scarlet anchored to
solitary biped far upstrand   controlling China!
closer to home   scattering   dry spume over recumbent
dreamers of bronze and gold   windmill child careens to the
      edge of
the known   spins   flings himself into   the surfcurl
"the silkin tent"   draws up to summer's noon
decrees Virgil   in the ascendant   elemental change
we too must take the plunge   into all that disorder and
      purpose
so we divest and pass   through other bodies   enter
immediate diverse motion   how we are instantly lifted and
      battered
our shouts lost   the din of spray   but gain the slower deep
support and buoyant float   and sport in surface ease
lavished by radiance of sound   our leitmotif
the burden of that light upon this sound

forgetting we are wavering over drowned
submariners   astrolabes   foremast of doomed   sailing
ships   prows driven into sea-silt   riding the glittering
height of our day   we shake off weeds that twist about our
    wrists
to drag us down   no no   that's not our sphere
we would not have it so   but this   effortless unfettered
in their trajectories do flying fish from rainbow arc regard
what spirals without haste in fathomed corridors or mark
the underwater upward gaze   of the young seaman's bold
    unseeing?

we make our sea scape   in full sight emerge   at the margin
Virgil with dignity advances   "Ancestor of Whales
Appears to Have Walked"   dwellers of shallow estuaries
also have their vocations   quickhands castling and tunneling
in meridian heat   the sky whitens   the bloom of the sun
the afternoon levels   we zero in on   our oasis   mirage
against the glare   exchange as tender   smiles
felicities of pique-nique   peripheral   ladies of perpetual
shades and the white   sacrificial calves   of fathers and
husbands out of actuarial   offices   less than a mile up
guardians of life survey from towers   coveys of shore-
skimming girls on burning sands   singleted heroes leap and
    run
under the little plane's redundant banner   course elliptic
drone WILL YOU MARRY ME MARY LOVE CHARLIE
Ludmilla's future
calls her name from rolls of shrimp-pink substance cased in
    strained
Lurex   she   pregnant and loose-topped   toddles her son
tips him in   the briny   out there   sails dip like sleeves
of novices   beyond   the thread of the steamer unravels
the myth of horizon
we open novels
later the light on the water   what is the motive of the light
changes   cerulean to plum towards   emerald gathering the
    wave

heaps itself   glassy curve   crescent   breaks and falling
sweeps its unfurling peacock blue   signal   the chariot
      descends

she flows towards us   dea incessu patuit   simultaneously
men women children   frail mortal frames   transformed
luminous obelisks   moving beneath a firmament   the sea
      reflects
violet wimpling   empurpling dusk   starry benediction
she bestows murmuring   it is time   all the time in the world
glances poignant with sense   the day's eye darkened
the eye of the wind   shuttered   the strip of land
nearly deserted   we collect our belongings   what we have
      left
inadvertent   rings coins metal of any kind   will be found
by night detectors   we turn reluctant   one last look
she urges   say not   wordless   how it is certain
we must die   but wordless think   we have been happy here

LOOKING-GLASS DAYS

Summer's gardens dead, or dying
    leaves of summer fled, or flying,
        and over the marshland the curlews,
        crying, crying.

Oh, in those other days!
        So numerous were the throng of friends
that all the piano nobile was opened where the Summer
Exhibition hung.

How the fine weather held, time out of mind and long past
    reason.
Heats and swoons. Silkin sails. Beneath those other skies
we moved within complicities of praise.

Such parasols, such frills!

Never were we severe in our pursuit of pleasure. Novels in our
    eyes,
we read volumes. Even the fireflies punctuated dusk.
    Mornings,

blue flash of wit. But it was noons we loved. One night the
    moon's
cool touch on our shoulders made us turn our heads.
    Sun-laden
under white netting, apricots ripened—"Now you must tell
    me everything."

From the maze: "And if we are parted a thousand years my
    darling—"
Should we have known? Heard the dog's drowsy bark, the
    cricket's clack,

the fall of a single petal as distant thunder?

When the downpour began and upstairs in darkness came
the terrible sobbing out of the room at the end of the hall,
and the voice, "You know nothing about me, nothing,
          nothing at all,"

we saw the gardens drown, the great house founder,
the ivy ripped from the wall, the statues toppled. Blinded,
the looking-glass, the hundred-stringed lute

split, its keys scattered like rinds on the carpet,
the backs of the books broken like vertebrae,
the porch torn off like a sleeve.

After-dawn's chalky finger wrote the auctioneer's mark
on the ceiling, the wardrobe, the branches outside the
          exhausted windows.
We rose pale from our pillows. Nothing would be the same.

Still in our nightwear, we ventured (that room was sealed).
Daring the clock's dry whisper, descending the well
to untenanted kitchen light, barefoot we crossed the sweet-
          grass

matting, pushed the screen, entered the lawn's arena: strewn
chartreuse turbans from the tulip tree, the down-drooping
          laburnum's
envious bruised clusters—

the dial's gnomon not ready yet to speak with its metal tongue.
Lumen me regit vos umbra.

At the little fern-lipped pool, stooping we dipped our hands to
          scoop
messages flung by the weeping birch, white motions of our
          arms,
wrists, fingers replicating swans' sinuate dipping. The mirror

rippled, settled, cleared.
We bent to meet each other's human guise.
Exchanged the colors of consummate gaze. Oh, name!

Our real past held in that deep, cool palm, we could imagine
coins of that realm pressed on thin laminae of flesh
over our vision at the second of our deaths.

In violent calm, we stood and turned away,
exiled from those bright waters to another season.
Passed from ivoried happiness through gates of newly
      polished horn.

WINTER CROSSING

1

In January, Venus dominates,
low on the western horizon at sun's set
over the farewell city. We leave her there.
(We take the idea of her with us like an icon
stowed with our gear.) Lifting off, wheels thudding up,
music bubbles, garbled. We are belted in.
We receive instruction. It is like the first day
of night school There are whistles we may blow
to attract attention should we set down on water.

2

Soon, we are brought drink; later, food.
We may rent headsets. There are magazines.
We may smoke, in the section. We do not know
each other, yet affinities might rise
to be recognized, for we may now
move freely about the cabin. Eight hundred eyes—
some may be glass, four hundred noses, how many
capped teeth, trusses, marks of identities
dear to their bearers—in this cetacean sounding
depths above the firmament, far from Spain.

3

In Madrid last summer to study Inquisition
documents, in the Prado a friend met an Irishman
old enough to be her father. *Coup de foudre*.
They looked no more at pictures. Since, every day,
every day a letter to her in Maine. He sent

a silver snake in the shape of a bracelet from Greece
where he went for a short spell with his English wife.
Worn by transatlantic tenderness
my friend's narrow, clever face; her wrist, more thin
supports the sleeping circlet. She agrees,
to be cherished, not punished, is to be desired.

4

But we are not flying to Spain. When the lights go out
for the feature film ("Now we all look alike.")
we find ourselves on an Arctic expedition.
So much whiteness, such terrific wastes,
glaciers, crevasses, frozen cataracts!
Bijou adventure. ("The dark one—is he the villain?")
Below us, imagine domed pilgas, hearts of blue ice.
The sledge flies over the glittering plain, the hero
urges his team faster, faster, but the villain
eludes, and starts the fatal avalanche.
The persistence of vision. Coldest is blue ice.

5

After these distractions, we try to sleep.
The attendants give loosely woven blankets out
to their charges. We are very good. Tucked in,
we attempt to compose ourselves as best we can,
but our heads are restless on the little pillows.
Shut away from clouds, up near the cabin roof
the dreams are murmuring among themselves.
Our watches are at odds. ("Oh, what is the time?")
Everywhere, down there, the clocks, the flails, the escape-
    ments.
In this queer middle realm, time's out.
Down there, someone is waking at first light.

6

Each passenger must complete a landing card.
Cards are collected row by row. Our names
will be known, our various destinations.
The captain's voice reports that the temperature
on the ground is mild, the weather overcast.
We raise our shades. The sky has seen everything.
We are preparing our approach under orders:
safety belts re-fastened, trays made secure,
seatbacks upright, smoking materials extinguished.
Hands folded. No talking. . . . We make the final turn
like a dowser's wand towards the right place, the spring.

7

Borne like a vessel down a nave of stars,
rushed on the new moon's hook through the river's dark
flying the long arc Eastward over seas
blacker than eagles' wings, the field of our crossing
blacker than poplar groves littered with bright shards
transformed to archer's arrow, argent serpent,
swan that came out of the dark at the edge of the flood
to the light of our windows and we rose as one
to view his coming, white on the black river waters,
in that commotion, calm, his uncrested head
inclined as if to receive a chain or crown,
we arrive at the source of our being, the dawning shores.

BETWEEN THE WORLDS

1

In music is relief of silence.
Pause is to stress as light to shade.
What is a shell but incremental echo?

Distances inform the spider's web.

If, on opposite shores,
lights seem at night to tremble,
the cause is impurities of air.

Do we seek to comfort the waves of the sea,
assuage the griefs of mountains?

One must think death
least of all things.
The last thing we thought of
was silence.

2

Some days the music comes badly,
jangle of metal strings.

Animals return to hill and tussock,
trees retreat. Stones remain
stones.

In the sky,
birdsong, thin coins.

Languid estuary
waters fall in pleats like a woman's dress,
the dress of a woman taken in sleep
to another existence. Has she learned
to see in that dark?

Some days the music does not come at all.
No music's sound is silence.

3

Then it was he invaded my eyelids
and rapt me away as I slept,
led me down the dark path
turning from time to time
to see that I followed,
white shadow of his shade,
eyes pale stones staring.
When we passed, the coven of poplars
rattled thin leaves blacker than the air
where bats twittered like darting orange-fish
in the coral groves at home,
domain of my changeable father,
he who warned me not to marry
that teacher of ceremony to mountain oaks.
Among these steeper mists, might memory fail?

4

Oh, single device of my heart!

5

We came to the heart of earth,
the river gray as a street in rain.
The crazy craft wobbled into the current,
he put an arm out to steady me,
I wanted none of it, but stood

an upright statue in a boat of tears.
On the other shore, he left me
no word but gesture.
Tall, drooping beside pools,
white cypress, white aspen greeted me like sisters.
Alone, I mounted the shallow steps,
entered the palace reared of clay
in whose vast red chambers
moist breath beat like wings.

6

I could have told you of the heart.
How at first it swells, bruised, dis-eased—
dishonored in its small red cave,
how it beats against constraint,
an instrument pleading to play,
a throat longing to sing.
How, later, it shrinks to the size of a husk,
unable to recall embodiment.
Under such conditions do we live.

7

This, then, the difficult passage
you descended, folded in dusk,
your captor now and again glancing back
to see that you followed, your eyes
pale stones in a grave sad face,
fair shape a shade on the iron road,
footsteps vanishing in ghostly wake.
When the invisible begins to stir,
the rocks to quicken, the ravines to pulse,
trees startle like deer, pools well with joy,
the aspen tremble and the cypress smile,
the palace looming behind you
shall you hear and know unfaltering
my hand has struck the strings

releasing springs of the world, and we ascend
following the thread of dark to recognize
the light of ourselves? I just turning my head
to look over my shoulder—
all that is to come.

EXILES

1

The steeple misses heaven, and the rhinoceros
dreams of France.
A needle would travel around the world.
Does the reflection of it long for light?
A letter from a foreign country: the successful
fugitive has already crossed
the next border.
Blue shadows of China
under New England eyes.

2

Sailing to Borneo,
where she will wed the young missionary,
a young woman stands at the rail,
one hand shielding her gaze against the glare
of the beloved face she scarcely,
after two years, remembers.
"Now it is all beginning at last,"
she thinks. Elmfield seen no more.

3

Suspended from the ceiling of the *farmacia*,
floating above the sea of elixirs,
tinctures, tisanes, the mummified
crocodile.
         Of what use to him
tintura di murra, antiscericum, the herbal liqueur
that ensures good digestion and long life,

stomatico di lunga vita—
far from the Nile?

4

"Dear Mother,
Your order for 3/s 4d of Tuesday last
was very welcome as I
had been without food for 42
hours (forty-two). Today I am twenty
hours without food. Your order will keep me
Monday mid-day—then, I suppose, I
must do another fast. I regret this
as Monday and Tuesday are carnival days
and I
shall probably be the only one
starving in Paris."

5

All over Ireland in the sweet, dank night
bedroom window sashes are gently raised to permit
souls of the newly dead.

6

How many people realize
that the bones of King Edward the Martyr
for which a Russian Orthodox congregation
built an expensive shrine, are stranded
in the vaults of a bank in Woking?

7

"OLD TIME HORSES RODE BY ALL WITH JOY"

8

Down the steep stone stair—
oh, hundreds of steps—
between the churchyard and the other wall
the children in sandals and smocked
summer dresses descend with their shovels
and pails under regard of the clock
in the blue tower towards the golden sea.
Beneath the enormous sky.

9

Tall, narrow chimneys of factories
outside the town expel each morning
thin shafts of white smoke
trembling in keen air.
If the smoke rises straight,
the natives say the weather will
stay fair.

10

"Dear Charlie,
                 We are anxious to know
if you are happy in the spirit world.
How do you employ your time?
When and where shall we go
to communicate with you? Will you
write a message?"

11

A memory,
of rooms filled with light and flowers,
fragrance of women as flowers,
moving about the rooms, the ease and music
of it all, the conversations, laughter

like bird-flight, quick bright looks
like no others, in passing . . .

12

One does not mourn what one has not loved.

13

The great blue
tutelary of blue place
of waters that let in the darkening sea,
having stood long
in promontory meditation, one
stilted leg his prop, tilted
head seeming to listen for possible
whispers under the tide's loud susurrus,
decides: a second
downward extension, an awkward comic
balancing on his rock,
wind-struck
tent or blue umbrella—imago, origami
unfolding, lifting blue, air-borne,
aloft and levelling into steady flight,
slow-beating wings
bearing the body of himself across
the blue wall between opposing littorals,
making of home an exile and of exile, home.
And then in dusk become invisible.

PRELIMINARY STUDIES

A great-aunt bought herself a transformation.
Perhaps she thought her life would change.

Gainsborough saw broccoli in elms, and George the Third
took off his hat to a small pine tree, believing it
the King of Bohemia.

In the late development of the disease,
the cloud that covered his vision
changed to violet, a color
Borges detested.
                To the lowlier bee,
the dandelion appears purple.

Venetian laws against luxurious display
decreed black gondolas.
                   Across Honfleur sands,
Boudin's ladies float in gondolas of shade.

Out of the gilded coach
passing down Whitehall, looks of mild inquiry
at the curbed populace from three princesses:
tame, long-nosed horses at a gate.

Scriabin to a friend:
"Money fell on this letter.
Hold the pages by the edge.
The fourth page is not contaminated."

Monet to Bazille: "I've done
a lot of pictures—sea
views and figures, and gardens,

and what-not." On the road to Lauves,
a thunderstorm surprised Cézanne
sur le motif, and Renoir died
with the word "flowers" on his lips.
Life, death—"all the usual things."

The hand of existence on the face of art
fumbles, its fingers splayed and blind,
trembling against that terrible slow prescience
that bears all, and does not forgive.

The circumference of a wrist!
An arm's cubit—measurable.
But how explain the accident of form
coincident with grace?

Or how in answering of eyes
our selves, our loves,
we think we recognize
and so, burning with lies of the possible,
set out to revision of the world?

Was a woman whose lover looked elsewhere.
Her voice darkened and mottled,
her hair took on the hue of disappointment.
She ceased utterly to care
that Russian frogs are woken from hibernation
by thunder,
that mushrooms detected by the human eye
will cease to grow. What with sowing and plowing,
the peasants are more tormented than ever.

A leave of happiness . . . the return to the Front,
the Parade with its gay flags and gallant marchers,
day trippers breathing of the pure
ozone guaranteed by adverts, elderly couples
walking arthritic marriages, invalids
hooded and glassed, rare specimens in bath chairs,

strollers and striders, the shouter
rushing and shaking his fist in an ague of rage,
mute gentlewomen distressed
by foxes at their rusty throats
and the roar and swing of the Kursaal,
near the kiosk remnants in spats, of an age
when foam danced in spangles on the Côte d'Azur,
down at the shingle's rim
the little boy bailing the sea with a bucket,
the dog haunch-deep in the shallows
greeting the next wave, a new friend;
and not so far out as might be imagined
(the haze may confuse)
the young man in red bathing trunks trying a sailboard
and falling again and again into the aquamarine.
Alone at a café table
someone opens a letter of a foreign stamp,
effecting a shift in the universal perspective.
And those two standing motionless at the balustrade
against the foil—
luminous silence in that rendering.

Out of the picture,
on the knoll below the fortification,
the artist at his easel
makes light of his work.

TALES FROM HIBERNIA

Our heartland of winter you must not imagine
locked in a frozen embrace of ice and snow
behind closed frontiers, impassable mountains:
no, no—we who are citizens, native or naturalized,
can tell you, plenty of life is going on!
The hare, large ears haloed in hoarfrost,
springs over the staunch white meadow
traced by the shadow of the eagle's wings;
in the forest the brisk-tailed wolf
tracks the deer who, turning its branchy head,
widening the cups of its nostrils,
hesitates; upright in its hollow nest,
the stoat, dainty in ermine, nibbles
the mouse it has just compressed in its claws.
And all is domestic and merry.

Blizzards swarm out from the white skep,
the bear in his fastness snores
like a dog in a sunny dooryard.
Lanterns like glowworms appear on the trails
as the men search the screes and creavasses
for the traveller caught in the storm,
and when he is found, form wavering
illumination on either side of the box-sled
winding the dark between enfilades of trees.
At the very same time, in a village cottage,
its eaves hung with long-toothed icicles,
the grandmother, bedridden, dreams of a bridal,
the grandfather, still spry behind his lids,
of the legendary summer of the mermaid—
here, we make up our own minds.

From the bulging cloud issues the föhn
to rush through ravines, unnatural wind of the south.
Under the ice, the river is all eyes,
and a mouth that can open anywhere,
as for instance on the light footfall
pressing its lips and the child is taken,
a trinket, a keepsake.
Now forever the drowned
one will be the wunderkind
the others can never live up to.
For the father, the first-born,
for the mother,
all of her life was saved for this moment.
Later, in the village, a rime of bells.

Although we may be temporarily
perplexed, we do not despair.
When the glacier passes the window with her long glissade,
we indoors ignore her and turn
like sunflowers to the pet crow
perched on a corner of the kitchen-altar,
from his yellow beak spelling in jagged syllables
stories to us of years ago.
Thus we spend many pleasant evenings.
Indeed, we are going on splendidly.
The watchman carrying his "Morgenstern"—
a ponderous club with spikes in the head—
calls the last hour. Safe in our featherbeds,
on clear nights we can hear the creaking
of wagon-loads of stars on the roads of sky.

Here is a story for you!
Very early one morning,
before the aurora has faded,
hooded and cloaked
a girl steps over her window-sill
straight onto the snowbank
and, with a single glance

at the blank cottage behind her,
sets out across the tree-tops
for the next village. She has an errand:
under the hinge of her basket
hide dozens of Alpine roses
carved through the endless year
by the whole family down to the youngest,
the unsmiling boy.
These she will sell to a cunning tradesman
who puts pins in their backs for the ladies.
So hard is the crust of snow
she traverses she leaves no imprint,
though on the windless air
her breath inscribes frost flowers.
At last, this coldest dawn,
she begins to descend the hill
to the village street, at this hour
still deserted, laid flat
by the giant roller. From a few chimneys
pipe thin blue reeds of smoke.
                              Nearer,
a sleigh blocks the little humped bridge,
the horse standing patiently with its white blinders.
And the occupants, bundled in furs,
his gloved hand gripping the reins,
she sitting upright beside him,
how they are motionless.
Closer, she sees
that they do not, but to her living eyes
return marvellous stares.
Over the ridge the sun rises
without wonder, since there is nothing new.
Beauty is everywhere, not least in winter.
When she goes on, she has something to think about.
She clatters the bell of the dark-browed door
and enters the shop where the merchant is waiting.
She opens the faithful basket, and there!
the shop is filled with the fragrance of summer.

"Well and good," says the merchant. "A clever conceit."
But spying the actual roses—
yes, this is the real surprise of the story,
and I shall leave it to you to interpret—
the merchant is quite out of countenance.
"I can do nothing with these,"
he says. "They do not at all suit the purpose."
"Be off at once," he cries,
"and do not show your face again."
The end of the story is not yet,
but that is the lesson of roses in Hibernia.

IN THE AQUARIUM

At the first display in the glass-domed rotunda
resounding with voices magnified yet dissolving,
a placard acquaints the casual visitor
with the fact that a fish is an aquatic vertebrate
possessed of a simple heart.
The viewer,
standing on two legs amid a shoal of tourists
before the transparent barrier
between air and water,
can easily assimilate the information
together with a name Adam never knew.

In a reasonable facsimile of their native habitat,
these large, smooth-bodied fifth day creatures
the color of blue clay travel solemnly
circling in slow motion frames,
or hang,
heavy as sash weights,
horizontal.
They stare, but not in wonder.
Wonder is not communicated in their turn,
nor curiosity, nor disdain.
Simply, they exist
immersed in the history of their element.
A fish out of water cannot live.
The bespectacled observer strolls on,
even as the archaic eye comes round again.

In vaporous light a long way down
from the dome of this Palace of Memory,
creep the crustaceans,
chitinous, calcareous,

eyes out on stalks,
canes like antennae tapping signals of intent
in response to a single stimulus,
stiff-jointed under their exoskeletons
but able to navigate unaided
by orthopedic arthropodan devices.
Elderly carp in toques.
swathed in ancient liberties, negotiate
accustomed channels with the complacency
of species protected by the Crown.
Seated at his usual table
a little removed from the flow,
the antediluvian
tortoise deliberately seeks
discreet refuge in his daily *Times*.

Flanked by immemorial potted palms,
the esecutore at the keyboard of the grand
sprinkles out tunes of sixty years ago,
occasionally rewarded by the faintest humming
as of insects in dry summer grasses.
Phrases of reminiscence
insubstantial as seasmoke
rise and drift above marooned coffee cups
and broken shells of meringue,
twine about architrave and pillar
garlands of tribute to the half-remembered
passionate unwithered heart.
I thought, If he doesn't ask me, I'll die.
The family, of course, were against it.
I could refuse him nothing.

"They told us a fete,
but really it's only a jumble."
At Bella Vista,
                    the past has sunk
to the bottom of the pond's green murk,
the croquet ground lies deserted,

the dainty, useless pavilion
beckons in vain. At the main house,
in the solarium, are exhibited
the spectres at a feast of bits and pieces,
flotsam flung up by the tide for the pickers,
flawed knickknacks, one-time treasures
chipped, cracked, or crazed, discarded
ornaments among the nemesia plants,
the damp-spotted books, the frayed velvet boxes
laid out on trestle tables dressed in white paper,
presided over by glazed smiles.
Takers of chances may choose
to guess the antique doll's name—
she who sits propped for inspection,
her gaze a vague glare, her teeth perfect—
Maisie, Venetia, Cora, Pearl?
Find the semi-precious hidden gem,
win the mystery prize.

Within those glass walls,
the air was stifling. Out here
on the windy terrace, where the weeds
have begun their perennial invasion,
it's fresh as water, breath
of the atmosphere buoyant, invisible,
confirmed in clouds
streaming across the brilliant ground of sky,
the deprivation of which is death.
Nor is the immediate landscape vacant:
see, at the end of the blemished garden
how the two small figures of human persuasion,
sweet stains of green on their raiment,
tumble over and over down the grassy slope
turning beneath the sun's invigilating eye,
and, in the middle distance, anchoring
the earth, the tall fountains of trees.

BETRAYALS

i

"Ah, perfido! Perfido!"
sings the soprano piercingly,
and suiting the action to the word
seizes the dagger from the commandant's desk
where the death warrant has just been signed,
stabs the basso and in a jet of red
leaps from the open window. He dies,
she rises, brushes dust from her hands,
and arrives to join him for the curtain calls.
The theater of this drama is the world,

said Vecchi, the Vespucci of the form:
a play having most or all of its text
set to music, with arias, recitatives,
choruses sung to orchestral accompaniment,
elaborate costuming, scenery, effects—
an altogether ridiculous concept, surely.
How many people sing to each other for hours?
Then, there's the problem of garlic.
What time does the next swan leave?
At least, some might urge,

let the composer make the work
less demanding, send us home humming—
that's the ticket!
Beware of gypsy encampments,
tombs, mountain fastnesses,
forked lightning, escaping steam, conflagrations.
Resist the superb
diva with her resemblance to a funeral barge,

the heldentenor with huge, one-nippled shield.
Opt for a little *verismo*, at most.

ii

When the benevolence of nature was betrayed
by the Lisbon earthquake, Madame de Pompadour
wore no rouge for a week.
Rich skirt of dressing-gown drawn back,
Emperaire's body in the gaudy chair
property of the artist:
child's unbonneted knees,
hands like small animals in a *nature morte*.
So to the surmount of the splendid capital,
the brow resigned to suffering thought,
the eyelids half-awaiting coins,
the dark
dwelling eye familiar with the sleep
that does not come, that does not come.

iii

The faithless mist
lifts to reveal the islands, continents'
castaways. The turning wing
of earth rejects the day, and stars
deprive the night of anonymity.
The rounding moon
abandons abstract referents and takes the sky
prima donna assoluta,
globe, orb, overriding wonder,
luminary of tides and lunatics
before the inevitable eclipse.
All that we are begs beauty stay.
"Alas, my love, farewell, I must away."
Treachery's the stuff of every hour,
and every hour betrays the lyre's voice

which can't be anything but true.
False smiles, chicanery, disguise,
forged documents, messages in unbreakable codes,
eyes and ears jostling at keyholes,
names spoken, the one name unspeakable.

iv

The innocent ward of the black-clad uncle
who tutors the handsome, young philosophical student,
incognito heir to the neighboring kingdom,
with whom she has fallen, of course, in love
in the way of *gemütlich* operetta,
after a glance about to be sure
she is not observed, retrieves
from her dirndl bodice the sealed letter
delivered by stealth before dawn
she has been saving till now,
the letter, she sings, of declaration
that this very night they will be together,
ah, bliss, she sings, and kisses the envelope,
then, humming a phrase of her later rapturous
aria we have come to expect,
crosses diagonally to the writing table,
takes up with a flourish of joy the paperknife
and slits

the set of limitations which contains her heart.
Out rushes a scarcely recognizable voice:
"Perfido! Ah, perfido!"

This turn of affairs pleases no one—jeers,
catcalls, the bewildered composer
is booed from his loge, tomatoes rain
from the gods,
the orchestra sinks in chagrin,
the conductor waving his little stick in vain.
The impresario tries to calm the hysterical singer,

who has launched herself at his throat,
raving that he is a charlatan,
which he undoubtedly is, but one does not
spit in his face. The curtains clash
like cymbals, and the rest of the rout
brawls towards the box office,
demanding its money.

TREASURES

i

The Sloth

Behold this sloth, caged representative
of the arboreal mammal whose genus in natural habitat
lives entirely up in the air among the processes
of photosynthesis and transpiration. At rest,
which is usually, they hang beneath branches
                               back downwards,
clinging with hook-like organs
to which the terminations of their limbs
are reduced.
Loth
to descend to earth,
they travel higher paths,
algal green along slow avenues,
to feed on leaves, succulent shoots, recalcitrant
tropic fruits gathered by mouth,
boughs dragged by forelimbs; passing from tree to tree
nocturnal, quiet, inoffensive, solitary.

Transported to day's light,
this sloth
in its glass house
smaller than life
in its slender gilded cage
on the illuminated page
bordered by paradisaical
vines with their perched
brilliant flowers,

bowered
before the public eye
that narrows down green centuries,
making eternal lunch of a lengthy twig,
for all the world as if unobserved,
retiring, tranquil, virtuous, illustrative
suggests revision of the catalogue.

ii

The Relic

Not of her,
virginal treasure-house
through whom heaven prevails, angels are made glad,
devils expelled, the tempter overcome, and the fallen
raised up,

not of her, declared pure
after trial by water in the ordeal of the Lord,
to whom an entire
fresh-springing month is given, whose images
retain utmost utility,

to whom Narses looked for direction
on the field of battle, whose likeness
Heraclius bore on his banner, although her assumption
is mentioned as doubtful in the capitularies
of Charlemagne; but of the other,
this object of veneration
once at home in its dark, perfumed cavern,
one among twelve particulars of its kind
common to vertebrates of the kingdom,
now set high in its miniature transparent temple

fit for gem or ivory, that the devout
might admire durability and structure

eminently suited to original function:
this relict sister in enamel habit,
the purported tooth of Mary Magdalene.

iii

God

Without denomination is described
in the Sistine manifestation
by an early anonymous witness:
"an old man in the middle of the ceiling
who is represented in the act of flying
through the air." Contrariwise
in Dublin, whose citizens are fond of labels,
God at the National Museum
is in on the ground floor
at the bottom of the case.
He is about three feet tall,
a chopped tree bole rescued from a bog,
heaved and hewn, the old reminder
in his blackthorn robe, stuck here,
seated, knees apart, on a sort of stump.
He shrugs, palms out towards the stooping viewer.
"What will you?" He seems to be asking.
"What did you expect?

iv

Miracles

Just as mirages in the sky,
effect of light waves from a distant source
bent and focused as they make their way
through the gravitational
field surrounding a cluster of galaxies,
may not be so rare as once thought
but are more abundant in the universe
than had been supposed, astronomers

citing five and possibly seven of these arcs
indicative of halos binding sheaves of stars,
so incidence of miracles appears
on the ascent in frequency, the wires
tingling and twanging from all stations,
Medjugorge, Toledo, Zacatecas, Torquay,
with visions, messages, phenomena—
odor of roses, spinning crowns,
doves soaring in formation, silver chains
turned to gold. Pilgrims converge
at every site by thousands,
hundreds in wheelchairs, hundreds on crutches,
invalid tourists wanting radiant signs.
At the edge of the scene,
buses and trains pant like dragons.
When the sun breaks through,
many of those assembled shriek, pray, point upwards,
crying they see—
Others, including a group of priests, stand by,
craning their necks but seeing nothing.
On two moons of the planet of Heaven,
satellite photographs reveal
volcanoes of ice, the first in the solar system,
whose glaciers vein the broad rift valley floors.

v

Hours

"Only to walk about and look at things";
primary pleasures
of these figures
in a landscape of natural flowers,
tree, insect and creature life, butterflies, birds,
including the cuckoo, not heard since France.

Essences animate this air,
of amaranth, marguerite, companula, bridal wreath;

from husks of priory walls
tendrils of ivy signal,
and in the mossy graveyard
the sexton leans smiling on his spade.

Below the altar of the grassy terrace,
the meadow with its straying tracks
descends to the river gaily persuading
children onto its stepping stones,
as guardians watch pensively from shore.
Midway,
the leading girl stops,
turns
to see how far she has come,
turns,
and, seeing how far she has to go,
wavers. The river rushes among the stones.

Her followers halt; some in the rear go back,
but she,
steadfast in terror, perseveres
at last to gain with triumphant leap
safe ground! (None so brave
as those who have no choice.)

Across the footbridge with its gripping-rail,
a drove of cows couchant on a field of green
surveys the moving human forms
wandering, errant, certainly striding;
over the wood, ring-doves wheel,
reel of platinum wings gold-strippled.

Dappled human voices, far caw of rooks,
amorous note of missel,
whispers of cloistral bells
make compliant consort, to which the horned snail
listens transfixed upon its gilt-tipped sprig.
In the middle distance,

near the frame's twining oak leaves, two beings
hover enclosed in their own sphere
of speaking silence, looking simply
at the same things at the same moment.
O treasure incorruptible:
ring of silver; circlet of bright gold.

C O L O P H O N

The text is set in Galliard, a type designed by Mathew Carter and Mike Parker, founders of Bitstream. The poem and part titles are set in Melior, designed by Hermann Zapf.

Composed by Books, Deatsville, Alabama.

Printed by the Princeton University Press, Lawrenceville, New Jersey on acid free paper.